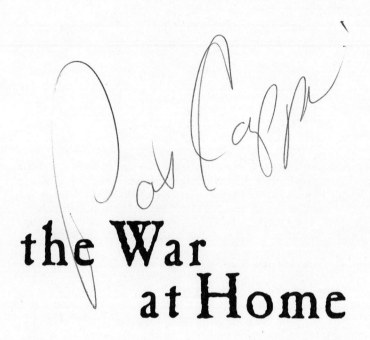

the War at Home

at Home

AN INTIMATE PORTRAIT OF CANADA'S POOR

Pat Capponi

VIKING

VIKING

Published by the Penguin Group

Penguin Books Canada Ltd, 10 Alcorn Avenue, Toronto, Ontario, Canada M4V 3B2

Penguin Books Ltd, 27 Wrights Lane, London W8 5TZ, England

Penguin Putnam Inc., 375 Hudson Street, New York, New York 10014, U.S.A.

Penguin Books Australia Ltd, Ringwood, Victoria, Australia

Penguin Books (NZ) Ltd, cnr Rosedale and Airborne Roads, Albany, Auckland 1310, New Zealand

Penguin Books Ltd, Registered Offices: Harmondsworth, Middlesex, England

First published 1999

1   3   5   7   9   10   8   6   4   2

Printed and bound in Canada on acid-free paper   ∞

CANADIAN CATALOGUING IN PUBLICATION DATA

Capponi, Pat, 1949-

The war at home: an intimate portrait of Canada's poor
ISBN 0-670-88244-5
I. Poor — Canada. 2. Poverty — Canada.
I. Title

HC120.P6C364   305.569'0971   C99-930522-0

Visit Penguin Canada's Website at www.penguin.ca

DEDICATED WITH THANKS TO:

Paul Quinn

Nora McCabe

Reva Gerstein

Diana Capponi

Joey Slinger

June Callwood

Cynthia Good

Ernest Hirschbac

Bev Slopen

Meg Masters

Scott Sellers

Julia Capponi

Catherine Marjoribanks

Elizabeth Gray

Cynthia Wine

Ellie Kirzner and the people at NOW magazine

Laurie Hall and the folks at A-Way Express

and to everyone whose story is contained herein.

CONTENTS

PROLOGUE

THESE DAYS, ACCORDING TO the National Anti-Poverty Organization (NAPO), the odds of a Canadian citizen experiencing poverty in his or her lifetime are one in three. And yet the majority of Canadians don't understand what poverty is, what it does to those who endure it, how it affects their children and their grandchildren.

We've been sold a bill of goods. Politicians at all levels assure taxpayers that they are being taken advantage of, that poverty, homelessness and addiction are just lifestyle choices made by those who simply choose not to pull their weight in society. Every report on poverty that briefly makes its way into the media is nullified by representatives from conservative think tanks who question the numbers, especially the income cutoff that is generally used to define the poverty line. Their analyses are calculated to leave us with the comfortable feeling that those who speak out on behalf of the poor, who represent these "special interest groups," are activists and doomsayers who are selfishly exaggerating the proportions of the problem and making excuses for those who "abuse" the social services that hardworking taxpayers are expected to pay for.

Politicians echo and prey upon our fears and frustrations. Our cities are unsafe, they affirm. Our sidewalks are crowded with the homeless: they're in our faces, in our doorways, obstructing our entrances to businesses, interfering with the way we view ourselves and our sense of who we are as a people, as a nation. Children of the poor are armed and dangerous. And drugs are everywhere, seeping out of poverty's ghettoes and into the middle class.

If we don't get mad, we're led to believe—if that is not a pervasive, legitimized emotion—if we don't "respond severely," well then, we're left with guilt, and hopelessness, and most of all fear. So, all over Canada, we're getting mad.

We live in a democratic society, and so the governments that enact the will of the majority do so with an increasing awareness and sensitivity to the public's need to feel the absolute necessity of harsh measures, the rightness of a "tough love" approach to social assistance. We need to believe that the "deserving poor" will be exempt from hardship and cutbacks, and that those who've grown too accustomed to the "free ride" will be forced to work for welfare. Instead of making us feel guilty or greedy or non-caring, they tell us that we're right. We *are* being taken advantage of. And *they* are the ones who will fix it. Our capacity for self-deception, nurtured by those in power, is boundless.

Canada, we reassure ourselves, is the best place in the world to live—the United Nations Development Program has told us so, for the fourth year in a row. Those who can't succeed here, we believe, are not worth saving. I wrote this book because I wanted to dispel some of this national complacency. I wanted to show the reader poverty—specifically urban poverty—from coast to coast. I wanted to give it a human face.

Poverty is not just the outstretched hand or the figure slumped in the doorway. It's not just the single mother down on her luck in line at the food bank, or the street kid looking for a safe place to spend the night. It isn't always genteel or hopeful, the person who might turn his life around with a little well-timed, benevolent help. It's a face that, no matter how charitable we might feel, we would probably rather not see.

I've spent time in mental institutions. I've been warehoused in a large boarding home for deinstitutionalized psychiatric patients. I've spent long months trying to live on welfare. I've been hungry and desperate.

I've also seen the other side—successes, the respect of my community, the ability to pay rent and eat and ride the transit system—but poverty is a shadow I carry with me, a darkness that can swallow you up in the blink of an eye.

With funding from my publisher, starting in the summer and ending in early winter, I travelled across Canada to look at inner-city poverty. Governments across the country—it doesn't matter which party holds sway—are cutting back on social services and closing doors that once led to opportunity for some. Because, for decades, we've allowed our social service agencies to pick and choose their clients by developing narrow, exclusionary criteria, permitting them to bar the difficult, the demanding, the unpleasant and the addicted, we now have a permanent underclass of the desperately poor and disaffected. They won't disappear, though many of us wish they would. They suffer. And their children suffer, and then grow into their own angry, lost adulthood.

Those whose fathers who, instead of tucking them in at night, got into bed with them. Those whose parents were lost to addiction: alcohol or drugs. Those whose mothers were brought up in abusive situations and found themselves always choosing men to whom violence was more common than conversation. Those whose parents didn't stay in school, because of hunger or behaviour or difficulty learning, and whose earning power was subsequently sporadic and minimal, causing stress and despair.

Those whose communities are as grey and barren as their lives, those without hope.

What do we do with them?

This year (1998), the United Nations Convention on Economic, Social and Cultural Rights told us something else, something that has left us feeling much less self-satisfied. The Human Poverty Index, defined as a measure of "the denial of opportunities and choices most basic to human development," provides a way to get out of the endless back-and-forth arguments about how to define the poor in dollar terms. Based on figures from 1994, before the worst effects of downsizing and cutbacks could be felt, Canada rated tenth.

Welcome to the best country in the world. If you can't make it here, you can't make it anywhere. And it's no one's fault or responsibility but your own.

the War at Home

AN INTIMATE PORTRAIT OF CANADA'S POOR

CHAPTER ONE

Vancouver

This isn't my first trip to British Columbia. The first time I came, back in the 1980s, I stayed at the Empress Hotel in Victoria, gave workshops and bought spurs that jangled and caught on the wooden floors. I visited again in the early 1990s and was driven to speaking engagements in Burnaby, Langley, Port Coquitlam and Richmond. I also gave a couple of speeches at Riverview, a sprawling B.C. mental hospital.

In spite of what I'd seen and heard from survivor activists, I always saw Vancouver as a fairly civilized place—smaller, slower-moving than Toronto, certainly prettier, even in the rain. I thought I knew the city, its environs, and its secrets: the poor, the mentally ill, the addicted.

Vancouver would seem to have everything a person could possibly want or need. Except consistent sunshine. Once you've been there, it's hard not to wonder why, especially in winter, you've chosen to live in any other province. It combines a big-city feel with a small-town pace, and everywhere you look you are reminded that pavement and highrises and all such human constructions are inadequate latecomers, smudging what was once perfection.

Vancouver's downtown is grown-up, attractive and bustling: highrise office buildings, coffeeshops at every corner, good bookstores, clean sidewalks. There are breathtaking man-made constructions such as Canada Place, which is designed to look like a ship, though it's hard to make that out when you're standing right in front of it. Built for Expo '86, it now houses a hotel, an IMAX theatre and the city's World Trade Centre; it also offers spectacular views of the city and the harbour.

If a city has to be carved from the wilderness, from the rock and earth and trees, it is essential that it keep at its heart a memory of how the land was before, and Vancouver does that, with breathtaking vistas and acres of forests and mountains that reflect a supreme indifference to the goings-on of us puny human folk. It gives me the same feeling I get when I'm staring up on a clear night at a sky filled with stars, confronting and comforting me with the reality of how insignificant my thoughts, concerns and ambitions are, reminding me that I'm just one of five billion crawling across the face of this planet.

It's a city of contrasts. For instance, it is possible to enjoy high tea at a very civilized hotel before beginning the nine-kilometre hike along the sea wall surrounding Stanley Park—which I did with my publisher, innocently wearing very new (and eventually very uncomfortable) cowboy boots. It's an extraordinary walk, circling the wilderness of thick forests and the serenity of the waters. It keeps your eyes wide with wonder. And it's to the credit of the citizens of Vancouver that they successfully fought off moves to develop portions of the area in the late 1960s and early '70s.

For me, of course, it comes naturally to wonder how many individuals are living in the densely wooded, wild areas; no one I asked would admit to knowing.

I am a city person, absolutely; it's in my blood and my being. My life has been divided between two of Canada's best, Montreal and Toronto; my exposure to the wild and the untamed has been limited to downtown streets after dark, to the predators and the prey locked into nightly Darwinian struggles out of sight of those whose more regulated, more civilized existence allows them to sleep with the confidence that morning will be waiting for them when they open their eyes.

If you ask people who've moved to Vancouver why, the answer is invariably: "It's the climate, stupid!" For me the city meant more than that—I had a sense that life here was gentler, more centred, that even poverty here in Vancouver could be endured with less agony than having nothing in downtown Toronto. The greyness, the ugliness, the sameness of the territories of the poor across Canada is mitigated here by the inability of local and provincial governments to rope off the spectacular vistas with user fees and dress codes and physical barriers. The wealthy and the homeless can both marvel at the ocean and the mountains and the parks, and feel a thrill of belonging and pride.

And maybe hope.

Many of the people who settled here originally came with nothing but their hands and a willingness to build, to create, to explore. Whether prompted by gold rush fever, the railway, fisheries or trade across the ocean, they came in search of opportunity, and stayed to build homes and raise families in the quintessential land of plenty. Needless to say, there have always been "undesirables"—the aboriginal people who found themselves overwhelmed and dispossessed by the settlers, and of course anyone non-white from other countries. But there is a new class of undesirables now—a homegrown class that I've come to see.

Holiday Inn, West Broadway

I WAS FIRST BOOKED into this hotel about five years ago, and I've grown quite fond of it. It has balconies, and I always, without asking, get the same view: the mountains looming in the distance, rising stark against the sky. Below me, I can watch people swim in all kinds of weather in the hotel's indoor pool. The street itself is a bit of a yawn—most places close in the evening, so there isn't a lot of foot traffic.

The neighbourhood is almost as familiar as my own home streets. Starbucks across the street, a doughnut shop and an A&W a block up, a huge drug store, and up the road is Greater Vancouver Mental Health Services (GVMHS), the agency that has brought me out several times to work with psychiatric survivors and staff. There are panhandlers strung out along the sidewalks—not too many, not too crazy, and not too aggressive.

As I was registering at the hotel the night before, still groggy from the self-medicating I have to do to allay the terror I feel whenever I fly, I overheard the desk clerk cautioning a young Asian man who was also signing in: "Our Chinatown isn't really safe at night. I wouldn't go there. Really." I asked the clerk where Chinatown was, guessing that it might be the very area I'm looking for.

This afternoon, I try experimenting with the transit system. I've been told by the helpful receptionist at GVMHS which buses to take—straightforward enough for someone born with a sense of direction, which I definitely was not. My destination is the downtown east side, specifically Main and Hastings, bordering Chinatown.

As I approach, having gotten off at the wrong stop, I see from a few blocks away what appears to be a mob milling around, as though an accident has just occurred—something terrible and messy and obviously compelling. Moving closer, revising my impressions, I begin to think that they must be gathered around the aftermath of a disaster, maybe an explosion—no one looks quite there. I want to stop a little distance away, just stare till everything's in focus, but I can't.

I keep walking forward, in a kind of shock. What is this?

Got to be close to a hundred people crowding the sidewalk. Threat is in the air; I can taste it on the back of my throat. Hard cases, all of them, men and women, black, white, Native, Asian. I haven't seen this many people on the street in one place all the times I've been in Vancouver. It doesn't fit what I know, what I feel about B.C.

Cement stairs lead into a great building, a city-owned and -funded community facility called the Carnegie Centre. I stand on the third stair, light a cigarette, try to look casually interested, try to take my bearings without staring. Two cigarettes later, I still haven't made any sense of it, and I'm starting to feel conspicuous. I decide to walk around the neighbourhood.

In one direction lies Chinatown. Colourful, neatly laid

out, with clearly flourishing restaurants and stores and no-smoking signs, it radiates prosperity.

Within a weak stone's throw is a police station, and all around are SROS, single-room-occupancy hotels: run-down residences for Vancouver's down and out.

> Brandiz Hotel
> Sunrise Hotel
> Balmoral Hotel
> Roosevelt Hotel
> Washington Hotel

Scattered between these buildings: CASH BUY AND SELL, ADULT XXX ALIBI PIZZA (out of business), CHEQUE CASHING, OWL DRUGS, boarded-up stores and open doors to ground-floor pubs in some of the SROS. The baked smell of beer and urine and too many cigarettes.

I wander back up Main Street, past a shattered bus shelter, looking for a place to land. In all the grime and defeat, there is one store that looks clean and organized. I go inside, hungry, and get an ice cream cone.

The owner has a few tables outside, in a kind of alcove. I stand there, on the edge of his property, eating the ice cream, watching the scattering of young men, in ones and twos along the street—easier to decipher than the mob on the corner. That they are dealers is obvious: they exhibit all the usual furtiveness common to the breed.

I watch as a clean-cut, apparently middle-class young man approaches one wreck of a dealer. At first I'm pleased—listening to the conversation, I think maybe he's an outreach worker from the Centre. Someone's trying.

"Hey, where you been? People been looking for you for weeks, how are you?"

The dealer can't get enough air in his lungs to be heard, though if he stood straight he'd probably be as tall as the healthy, vibrant, preppy-looking fellow addressing him.

"Do you have a phone number? No kidding, when you weren't in your usual place we worried, you know?"

When I see the money being slipped into the dealer's shaking hand, less than a yard or two from where I stand, I feel a sense of betrayal, foolish under the circumstances. Not a worker—a customer, a user. He fades as soon as he gets what he needs.

I'm a bit surprised at the openness. After all, the cops are housed within spitting distance. I want to know what's being sold.

I finish the ice cream and wander slowly, trolling, clearly looking for something. The dealer mutters to me.

"What'cha got?" I ask.

He's grey and bent, he smells and he's stoned. I catch the word *coke.*

I don't know Vancouver prices or slang: "I got twenty bucks, man. Coke."

He hands me a twist of paper in exchange for legal tender. I jam it deep into my pocket and walk back farther away from the intersection. I've been here less than fifteen minutes.

I'd known what I wanted to see in Vancouver, what I wanted to write about: the drug trade. I hadn't expected it to be so obvious, so much of an open-air drug market. I hadn't expected to find it right off.

I walk some bleak streets, eyes open, back tingling. Every alleyway is occupied—some with people shooting up, some so stoned it takes a group effort. Hookers. Crack-smokers in corners. Everything is furtive, every motion, every gesture.

Boarded-up stores. People passed out or just asleep. A guy pulls himself up, staggers over to a wall, pisses, collapses again. I feel myself scrutinized by some of the solitary watchers: prey or threat or opportunity?

There's a park of sorts, dying scrub grass, scattered benches, scattered people. Some are obviously out there, crazy folks spinning out the daytime hours. One or two heavies with heads together watch as I take a seat and light up. A man with slept-in clothes sits down with me, asks hopefully for a smoke, which I hand him and light. We chat a bit, and as we do I realize why I've stopped here. It has a bit of the feel of the psychiatric ward: a community of the bizarre and the lost. Some talk to the air, others stand too still; I have a feeling I'm the only stranger here. I'm told later that the underclass of dealers and users refer to the place contemptuously as Crab Park.

My friend accepts another smoke and tells me he wrote a story once, tried to sell it to Disney, a kids' story, want to hear it?

Sure.

"It's about a kid who won't eat his crusts. His mother all the time fights with him, but he does everything to avoid eating them. Mostly he hides them under his bed, 'cause he doesn't have a dog he can feed them to. So he keeps stuffing them under his bed until one night, all the crusts go through some magic process and become a monster that rises up." He stiffens his arms like Frankenstein's monster, hands reaching towards my throat. "And strangles him."

His hands twitch just a little at the ends of his arms, and I say, "And Disney didn't want it?" injecting some surprise in my voice.

"Go figure." He shrugs, dropping his arms.

We shake hands and I'm off again, heading back towards Main and Hastings.

This time I wade into the crowd, claiming a spot near a set of stairs cut into the sidewalk: although it looks like a subway entrance, it leads darkly down to washrooms, which I suspect no longer function. I have no intention of checking it out.

It's becoming clear that this crowd is not gathered at the aftermath of an accident. It is its own disaster, to which no ambulances race, no relief comes. A disaster bigger than the city that struggles to contain it, where neglect and abuse and poverty metastasize into drug addiction, prostitution, HIV/AIDS.

It might be my imagination, but I seem to be setting off waves of cold silence to my right and to my left. I'm a real conversation-stopper. I dig into my knapsack for a notebook and pen, then I pick a relatively harmless-looking guy, in worn Nike shoes, long hair and tattoos, to introduce myself to.

He refuses to give me his name, so we settle on "Nike," which seems to please him. Once we're talking together, the tension caused by my presence begins to disappear—so much so that we're approached a half-dozen times by men and women openly buying or selling a dizzying variety of street drugs. It becomes clear that this outside group is very separate from the Centre, which employs a very visible security staff to keep them out. Although Nike claims he doesn't "give a shit," he also curses the guards, and claims (probably falsely) that most of them are users too.

Nike's forty-seven years old, and he's been an addict since 1969. He says he uses needle-exchange programs, that he doesn't plan on getting hepatitis C or AIDS, although he's never been tested. He lives in one of the SROs in the neighbourhood, a small, stifling room like many others he's lived in over the years. It has a bed, dresser, sink and fridge, for which he (or welfare) pays $325 a month. He deals to pay for his own habit, a habit he takes some pride in controlling.

"I only shoot enough to take the edge off. I can still

maintain on those days that I can't get anything. I don't like anything running my life except me."

I ask about the proximity of the police station, why it doesn't have a chilling effect. He laughs and says the cops are everywhere but here.

He gets philosophical when I ask him if he isn't a little old for the life: "Life's what you make it, this is just as good as any other. You could be just as miserable in a mansion. Money's no fucking good unless you have some one to share it with." Somewhere he has six brothers and three sisters, even a wife.

People make their way through the ragtag collection of buyers and sellers here, calling out what they've got or what they're looking for.

Ts and Rs: the poor man's heroin, Talwin and Ritalin. Morphine. Coke (I should only have paid ten for the twist of paper sold to me by the dealer down the road). Tylenol 3s. Valium, 5s and 10s.

An addict's heaven, as long as he's got money in his pocket.

The morphine and other prescription drugs are provided by doctors, and Nike is a bit indignant about that—what they do is no different from what he does, but they're protected by their status. "And it's harder to come off pills than anything else."

Nike claims he was brought into the dealing life by a physical handicap: he's blind in one eye and losing sight in the other. He shrugs. "Nothing out there for a person like me."

I became aware of my first junkie when I was at college in

Montreal. He wasn't a student, just an entrepreneur looking for a place to sell his methadone so he could buy heroin instead. He said his name was Victor, and he always wore a dirty beige cloth raincoat, no matter what the weather. I forget how we were introduced, who I was with at the time. There were a number of dealers in and around the school, mostly selling soft drugs and the magic pink pills containing speed. One fellow, intending to go into law, carried his dope around in a hard briefcase, and his mother took orders for him over the phone.

We were doing a lot of speed and acid back then, as well as pot and hash. Late 1960s, early '70s—it went hand in hand with the times. My memory is understandably vague about details, but I do remember a couple of us standing with Victor by the blackboard in an empty classroom. He was showing us how to sterilize the needle, melt the pill in water, draw it up. He was injecting us, since neither of us willing to do it to ourselves, when fire bells started clanging and nearly resulted in three heart attacks. After the shock we continued, assuming it was a false alarm. Victor was just putting away his works when the door opened and these surreal-looking men stuck their heads in, outfitted in rubber coats and boots and helmets. They didn't see anything they shouldn't have, and we were able to look normal enough not to draw attention to ourselves.

Aside from that, it felt very good. Victor claimed that if you shot it, methadone was much like the real thing.

Perhaps a half-dozen times, different people and places: methadrine, methadone. It was way too good, and way too seductive. I knew I could happily drown in it. Some basic instinct for survival kicked in and I pulled back, stuck to LSD, Dexedrine and mescaline, taken orally.

A blond woman in her thirties, Maryanne, is trying to get rid of Percodan. She doesn't live downtown, only comes to work the corner. She shares a place with a girlfriend, a nice place, and she deals to pay for her own habit and the extras. Welfare top-up.

"Mostly this is the pill corner. Someone may want to get rid of two hundred Valium quickly, I'll buy them and resell for a profit. I'm good to my customers and they know it: only thing you have here is your good name, you know. If I sell twenty pills, I'll throw in a couple extra. Keep the customer happy."

She's scornful, most of the dealers on this corner are, of the crackheads.

"Coconuts," she labels them dismissively. "Pipes and needles. All they care about is doing some more rock. It's retarded. Never trust one of them. They'd sell their mother's wedding ring. See that guy?" She points to a head-down, shuffling figure. "They took him in the alleyway and beat the living shit out of him He ripped someone off, now his name's shit. I mean, some of these guys are really out there. There was a guy wanted to trade for a can of Raid. 'It's real good,' he says, and sprays his own face!"

She is frustrated that she can't collect a disability pension. "I told my welfare worker, if I had a needle in my arm, you'd put me on disability right away."

She'd quit the life if she could find work paying ten dollars an hour, even if it was digging ditches. Until then, she treats dealing like it's a job: going to work every morning, staying till her transactions are complete, then heading home.

She comes by her work honestly: she and her dad are "close as shit;" he deals in limited-edition art and pills. "We're a family of entrepreneurs."

I ask her if she has a phone number I can reach her at. She hesitates. Even though she's given me a false street name, she decides to take a chance. I write it down, including her caution not to mention drugs to her roommate if she picks up the phone. "She's religious, she doesn't know."

Use what you got is the philosophy here. Nike claimed that if he were a woman, he'd be "fucking like crazy, bringing in money hand over fist." I've met enough hookers who sell their bodies for ten bucks a throw not to get excited about this potential money-making scheme.

Oddly, none of the people I speak to believe themselves to be slaves of their habits. And no one feels any great moral quandary about selling, entrapping others. There is a kind of aggressive defensiveness about their business. Their slogan would be like the NRA's: *drugs don't kill people, people kill people*. Those who retain some hard-won control over their habits disdain those who can't. I suspect that scorn is fear-based, a kind of look into a very probable future.

This crowd of users and dealers is a community of sorts, with its own rules and its own rough justice. It can be hard to distinguish predator from prey: the only thing separating them is time.

When I get back to the hotel, I drag a small armchair out onto the balcony and just sit for an hour or so, my head filled with people and pain. It seems as though that one street corner has all the elements of poverty in microcosm. There are so many traps, and so few exits that lead anywhere. Especially now.

IN 1994, PAMELA FRALICK, then deputy chief executive officer and director of liaison and coordination for the Canadian Centre on Substance Abuse, went on an undercover drug buy and bust with some RCMP officers. She felt she was getting too far removed from the realities of the street.

A triathelete, she radiates good health and admits that she probably looked very out of place. I ask her what she wore for this adventure.

"No-name jeans. Runners, which I realized later were—even though they were old at that point—easily a hundred-dollar pair of shoes. A shell that was also well worn but that, as I was walking with the undercover cops, I remembered was Gortex, and therefore expensive and not usually seen. The police, more used to what makes for good camouflage, wore jeans and T-shirts and cheap runners."

They went out after dark, parked their car around the corner and walked up to East Hastings.

"It was like a party. The streets were really crowded, lots of people, and cars cruising slowly: some looking for drugs, some for sex, some just gawking. It took less than twenty seconds for us to be approached by a fellow selling. We were trolling for bigger fish, so my 'partners' just politely declined and we kept walking." That night there were ten or twelve undercover cops on the street. Two busts were made.

Pamela is particularly haunted by one event she witnessed.

"We were just standing around, and across the street two women were shouting and shoving at each other. My first instinct was to go and try to break it up, but the police said this was business as usual. The next morning on the news there was a report that a fatal stabbing had occurred where we were, a woman knifed by another woman, and I was afraid, still am, that that was what we were watching."

When Pamela returned to the station that night, she was struck by the businesslike mood of the officers, in sharp contrast to her own sense of the futility of their work. Without them, she believes, there would be no deterrence, no containment.

Pamela also went out with the Downtown Eastside Youth Activities Society (DEYAS) mobile needle-exchange unit. Clean needles, bleach, alcohol wipes and condoms are distributed from a van that makes regular runs and stops through the east side.

"When the van made its first stop, I wondered why, because it was a quiet, nondescript residential area. But in a minute or two, these very, very young girls started to come out of the shadows, most to pick up a new supply of condoms, some to exchange needles.

"If you looked up, you could see the diamond-like lights of the Grouse Mountain ski resort twinkling against the sky, a world away from this reality. When we hit the notorious 100 block section of East Hastings, with its carnival atmosphere, I had the strangest memory of the old ice cream truck pulling up on a hot summer's day. Instantly a line forms, and keeps forming, as addicts trade in their old needles for clean ones, more men than women, no one in great shape."

TODAY, THERE ARE MORE than 200 agencies operating in the Downtown Eastside, spending hundreds of millions of dollars. Result: 6,000 people in slum housing, epidemic disease and widespread crime . . .

Even the most conservative estimate puts Vancouver's addict population at more than 1,500. If you consider the shortage of decent housing, the situation is the same: staggering numbers in need. While it has poured huge amounts of tax money into the area over the last three decades, the city still lacks a sustained affordable housing program and a continuum of addiction treatment services.

—*Ian Mulgrew,*
Vancouver Sun, October 22, 1998

Back at the Carnegie Centre, I head for the front desk, where I find security—a big guy in T-shirt and jeans who looks like a bouncer. The receptionist is friendly, efficient and helpful when I ask for general information about the place. I might want to check out the writing group, she suggests. It's held on the third floor, at 2:30. I get a tour of the Centre and the programs offered.

Some good stuff happens here, if you can make it inside. If you're not scared off, like many who haven't been brought up in the street life. If you're not tempted to relieve your pain with the drugs on offer at the foot of the stairs, or the alcohol legitimately sold out of the first-floor bars of the SROs, all with doors open to the street, exuding the stink of beer and sweat and puke.

Nice people close their car windows and lock their doors when passing this corner; nice people get warned away. Nice people have sons and daughters who might well show up here, for a taste, just a taste. And some might never leave.

Carnegie is a two-million-dollar operation. Fifty-three full- and part-time staff work in the building. I ask Marilyn Sarti, the director, how it is possible to run programs with the crowd outside.

"It's extremely difficult. We try to keep out the dealers. Anyone caught dealing in the Centre is barred. The obviously intoxicated are also kept out. We have an appeal process as well—the security supervisor makes the final decision. I find the Centre much tamer than the last place I worked, heading up a Mentally Disordered Offenders program at the court-house."

She adds that, on occasion, some members of the security staff might be caught using on the job, but so far they have gone into rehab programs and been able to come back to work.

"We do various outreach programs, and trips—a number of three-day camping trips, day outings, that kind of thing."

"Have you considered working with the guys on the street?" I ask.

"There is a proposal for funding such an effort, we hope to hear soon."

For herself, she's quite interested in the scrub park and its inhabitants—the one dismissively called Crab Park by the dealers and users—which she calls Pigeon Park. She'd love to set up a storefront operation there, start involving those who have nothing going on in their lives.

I ask her what the general goal of all the programs run out of the Centre might be, and her response is: "To be the living room for the people of the downtown east side, to help people live healthier, happier lives."

Their seniors' program is very successful. Tellingly, they define senior as starting at age forty.

"Many of these people are single men, and some are vets. Some have sustained injuries on the job that means they are unable to work. Some of course have alcohol problems. Poverty and other circumstances mean many health problems, and people age a lot earlier in the downtown east side. They have nothing to do during the day. We have a pool room, a weight room, pottery and photography classes all going on in the basement. On the first floor there's a library, and its always full with people reading."

They have an advisory board made up of Centre users.

Frank Gilbert, of the Downtown East Side Residents Association (DERA), likes Carnegie, though he wishes some of its programs had a more immediate relevance. He worked for DERA in the 1980s, left the country for a time, and started back with them in the fall of 1995.

"Things don't change in this neighbourhood, except to get a little worse. Here I'd been away for almost a decade, and when I walked around, the same people I'd known back then were stopping me to say hello. Nobody here has the luxury of moving away."

DERA started out as a political organization, with a management board made up of people who live in the area. Its multiple-source funding comes from city, provincial and federal governments as well as charitable foundations.

Frank points out that it's centred in the poorest postal code in Canada, and, oddly, one of the only places in Canada where women's income is higher than men's, ironically due to the number of single women raising children on a social assistance allowance that's more "generous" than the amount single men receive from welfare.

"Here," Frank tells me, "we don't pretend to know all the answers, and our mission isn't to straighten people out. But if someone does decide it's time for them to get out of the cycle of addiction and poverty, we want to have something in place to offer them."

DERA's board and staff have come to the same realization as other grassroots activists across the country: that work—real, paid work—is a large part of the answer to poverty and the possibility of kicking an addiction. They are combining their efforts to hold on to low-cost housing, under threat of renovations and yuppification, in combination with employment opportunities. In partnership with a private investor, they've purchased a sixty-four-room SRO on the edge of Gastown. They are looking at business opportunities for downtown east side residents in building maintenance and recycling old beds by fixing the frames.

"The best example of business partnership has been our own landlord here at DERA. One of our guys was doing some painting for us, and the landlord happened to drop in, looked at the work, and said, 'This guy is good. I'd like him to do

some work for me.' We knew the fellow had a serious drinking problem, but we decided to shut up and wait to see what
would happen. Sure enough, he did good for two weeks, then
he took his paycheque and disappeared. This happened twice,
and the landlord actually sat down with him, told him:
'Look, I really want to keep you on, but there are times when
I really, really need you to show up. When I depend on you.
What can we work out?'

"So they worked out this system where the guy gets his cigarette and lunch money in an everyday payout, and the rest is
waiting for him when the landlord doesn't need him for a
week or two. It's an arrangement that works around the addiction, and manages to benefit both."

DERA, among other things, does housing referrals. They
have 7,500 names on their waiting lists, 84 percent of these
single males. They also started a voice-mail system for those
who can't afford phones, and after six months they already
have 500 subscribers.

IN THE SECOND-FLOOR cafeteria, I chat with David Paul Ross.
It's his birthday today, he compulsively tells everyone. He's
refused my offer to buy him lunch but accepts a coffee.

His left arm is paralyzed, but he's quite good at coping
with his right—I suspect he wouldn't appreciate anyone doing
otherwise simple stuff for him.

He lives in one of the SROs and he pays $350 a month out of his disability pension for a room with a hot plate, night table, wardrobe, bed and sink. No fridge. He buses the tables here, gets paid in meal tickets. Physically, he's a mess, having been kicked in the head while staying at a receiving home for foster kids, a kind of horse ranch. He was two. His left side was paralyzed—what are you going to do, it was a freak accident. He bears no grudges.

His natural parents already had eight sons and a daughter. "They gave me two things I really didn't want. Fetal Alcohol Syndrome and diabetes. Some going-away presents, eh? My natural father was English, like Captain Cook, and my mom was part French and part native Indian. I suppose they're dead now."

No one wanted to adopt a handicapped kid, so he stayed in different foster homes (nineteen or twenty of them). He liked the last couple he stayed with, and he's still in touch with them from time to time. "As a matter of fact, I phoned my foster mother yesterday. She wished me happy birthday," he beams.

He was sent to a remote residential training centre, to learn a trade. He calls himself a very ingenious person. He learned to compensate for his paralysis and became very good at furniture-making.

Bad luck kept dogging him, however. He got hit by a car, broke a leg, fractured his pelvis, everything on the left side got buggered up. He was air-ambulanced to Vancouver, kept in hospital for months, then sent to another rehab/training centre.

"The rehab centre found me a place to live, but it was the wrong place. Someone screwed up royally. I'm physically challenged: all they could find was a place that housed people just out of a mental institution. I didn't like it there. Why should I be lumped in with them? Got myself tossed out. You know, breaking the rules, coming in late."

The cafeteria, which wasn't too crowded to begin with, is emptying out. A mix of staff, volunteers and clients eat here, and one of them, at an adjoining table, has left a half-finished lunch of macaroni and sauce on his plate. David casually leans over and lifts it with his right hand, the left arm being mostly useless. He continues talking as he rubs the used fork against his jacket and digs into the leftovers. I make a conscious effort not to react.

"I should be in a small apartment, not just a room. A person could go stir crazy. I used to have a bike, I did pretty well with it, getting around, but it got stolen. Police don't care. They're more concerned with drugs. I never touch drugs. I've seen what happens to others. They go very strange."

He hasn't done very much on his birthday; he felt a bit unhappy.

"Not really lonely, more bored and a bit sad. Usually, when I have money, I go to a movie or do something else. I read, everything under the sun. And I like to talk to people, encourage them."

He's a nice guy, quite liked here, but an agency can't be a family, staff can't be friends.

UPSTAIRS ON THE THIRD FLOOR, the writing group is underway. They meet once a week, and everyone reads what they've got. It's quite a diverse group, fifteen people unlikely to talk to each other in the real world, and the mutual respect is touching. There's a street kid with an out-there haircut—he goes first because the youth food bank is open this afternoon and he needs to get some stuff. He never touches what he writes once it's done, just turns the page. It's hallucinogenic, choppy, sometimes nightmarish—probably mirroring his life.

There's a woman who's probably not: too tall, voice too deep. She writes of hopeful romance, with flowery language and imagery. She stands, as she reads in a clear voice, the others attentive and encouraging.

An eccentric man whose arms are oddly wrapped in strips of cloth, a few seniors, a few others who look like they wouldn't be out of place concealed at the end of a dark alley, waiting. There are prison short stories, edgy, with gritty realism in the dialogue and the characters.

It's hard to hear; other stuff is happening on the floor, people passing by, other groups meeting. But these writers are up to the challenge: trying to communicate as best they can with one another.

I take a walk around the building. The second floor has a room with a scattering of outdated computers. A few individuals are trying to crack what is to them a new technology, a new world. In the basement, a seniors' club—where smoking is permitted and coffee is free—is remarkably well attended. I wonder if they arrange to arrive in groups; I can't imagine they would dare to walk past the open-air drug market one at a fearful time.

I leave this place of industry and hope, however thin that hope is, and head back down towards the ice cream place, needing cigarettes. A couple of dealers, including mine, are strung out along the street, banished or self-exiled from the pill corner.

I watch one of them accept cash from a client who doesn't seem to be in much better shape. Here, in the shadow of law and order, crime and punishment, he looks for his stash. Tries one pants pocket, then another, then the back. He leaves them turned inside out, getting a little frantic—the transaction's turning farcical. He pulls off one ankle boot, hopping on the other leg as he peers inside, shaking it out. Off with the sock, the bare foot not much cleaner. Things are always in the last place you look. He finds what he's searching for in his shirt pocket, and the deal's concluded.

It's kind of like an end-of-the-world movie: the handful of survivors inside trying to rebuild, find some normality and acceptance and purpose, while at the gate the renegades, barely kept at bay, wait for strays.

I make my way back to the hotel. Tonight, the mountain, from my balcony, looks less majestic than it did.

Belatedly, I remember the street purchase I made, go back inside my room and retrieve the small twist of paper. I carefully open it—a fine white-grey powder nestles inside a strip torn from a BC-49 lottery ticket. Heaven and hell in one tiny packet. I wonder who makes up the packages; the guy I bought it from wouldn't be capable, his hands shook too much.

Cocaine has no mystery for me. No great lure. I wouldn't trade my life for it.

Not me.

ON THE PLANE OUT of Vancouver, I'm reading a report created by the Task Force into Illicit Narcotic Overdose Deaths in British Columbia. In June 1993, the provincial minister of health and the attorney general, under pressure after highly publicized overdose deaths, announced the appointment of the chief coroner to head up a task force:

> [The task force would] inquire into what ap-
> peared to be an inordinately high number of
> deaths associated with the illicit use of heroin.
> The media were simultaneously reporting that
> these deaths followed the distribution of welfare
> cheques toward the end of each month. Hence,

the headlines associating "Welfare Wednesday" with these events.

The final public hearing held at the Carnegie Centre in East Vancouver was originally scheduled for Thursday, May 26, but was postponed to June 9 because "Welfare Wednesday" was thought to have a negative impact on the May 26 meeting. Addicts are not alone in this world and they shouldn't be led to believe they are. When one examines all the social issues involved here, it boggles the mind. Where does it all begin, where will it all end? What is evident is that there are so many agencies and departments involved in all of these activities that one is led to conclude that this is an industry, with many who are perceived to be living off the avails of misery.

The chief coroner called for decriminalization of simple possession along with stiffer penalties for trafficking, as well as a heartfelt cry for coordination of government ministries and services.

Pamela Fralick, whose foray into the street scene five years ago still spurs her on, wonders what it is that prevents political or financial action to deal with the crisis, especially in light of all the reports and publicity.

"When I was in the downtown east side, in 1994, it all

seemed new and exciting, in the sense that here was a critical problem that we could have an impact on. Now, all these years later, we've failed to do anything but contain the horror to a six-block area. I think the situation has oddly normalized, we've accepted it as just another fact of life. The urgency has gone."

I get the *Vancouver CCENDU 1998 Report*, compiled for the Canadian Community Epidemiology Network, and prepared by Elizabeth M. Whynot, MD. Some snippets:

- Vancouver has a higher proportion of young adults than especially the newer suburban communities. Large proportion of the increase in population can be attributed to large migrations of people in the 20 to 29 age group into Vancouver.
- Vancouver/Richmond Health board has analyzed income data by community health area. The average income for residents on the west side of Vancouver is two to three times that of the north east sector of the city. The average income for that area, including the Downtown Eastside community so beset by the effects of intravenous drug use, is $9,331.
- City staff have estimated there are 6 to 7,000 single-room-occupancy units within the DES and adjacent communities, which are endangered by new development.

- The B.C. Provincial Coroner reports that, in Vancouver city, 151 deaths in 1996 and 141 (preliminary number) deaths in 1997 were caused by overdose of illicit drugs.
- In 1997, DEYAS recorded 256,278 client visits, with a total of 2,53,318 needles exchanged.

An article in the Calgary Herald on July 23, 1998, written by Jim McNulty, is even more chilling: "In Vancouver, 116 people died from overdoses between January and June [1998], 38 more than died in the first half of last year."

East Hastings and Main represents our social services in stark microcosm. Those whom we don't know how to help are kept at bay, left to drown in their own need. Those we find more acceptable we try to make comfortable in the emptiness of their lives; we create expensively staffed "living rooms" where time passes and lives ebb without ever fulfilling the human potential we all have.

We can't see that potential. Poverty and sickness and dependency obscure it. They steal lives.

CHAPTER TWO

EDMONTON

Crown Plaza

I WASN'T SURE TILL I landed whether or not I'd been here to Edmonton before. But where I'm staying is within sight of the Hotel MacDonald, where I spent one night on my last book tour: a hotel so upscale it's frightening. It overlooks the North Saskatchewan River Valley, an awesome vista allowing the weary traveller to gaze on the best face Edmonton can offer. Whoever booked me in probably thought it would be a nice treat for me, and though I appreciated the thought, I was afraid to touch anything for fear of leaving fingerprints.

The Crown Plaza's no slouch either, but on a more human scale. I'm still depressed from Vancouver. I want to go home and hide—not deal with people, not think about poverty or drugs or wars.

At least I have no emotional connection to this city, no preconceived notion of what it is or what it isn't. Maybe that makes it a good choice for this trip. I have a whole wall of windows in my room, and I open the drapes and stare glumly down at the traffic and greenery. It's been pouring rain off and on, a sea of grey clouds just now breaking up. I have to unpack, get some food, make some plans. I don't know anybody here. I'll probably check through the phone book for agencies and food banks, but not now.

Let's face it, I'm ripe for omens, for signs, for reassurance. And sure enough, as I stare listlessly out, a rainbow appears—not just an ordinary rainbow but a double one. I bang my forehead against the glass that I've forgotten is there, trying to get closer, not quite believing it. But there it is, it's real, and I laugh. I've never seen anything like it before—it's breathtaking.

I offer a small prayer of thanks to whoever's listening, for the lightening of my soul, and begin the tedious process of unpacking my scuffed and battered knapsack. What the hell, with a start like that, how bad could this experience be?

ALBERTA. THE LAND OF self-sufficiency, at the cutting edge of welfare reform, and the first province to adopt an Orwellian "doublespeak" labelling to mask its intent.

Just as the federal government has given Unemployment Insurance the new, more enthusiastic, go-getting name Employment Insurance—a term that disguises stiffened eligibility requirements and shorter pay-out periods—Alberta has put a more genial face on its welfare system by calling it Supports for Independence.

I leaf through the tourist magazine *Where*, which highlights the sights and happenings in Edmonton for the summer of 1998. An unsigned article entitled "The Business Traveller" cites a piece published in *The Globe and Mail*'s *Report on Business* that names the city "one of the top five business centres" in Canada. It also claims: "this dynamic city's high quality of life comes at a remarkably low price tag. Edmonton residents enjoy lower living expenses, taxes and housing costs than people in most other major Canadian cities. There is no provincial sales tax and the basic income tax rate is among the lowest in the country. The per capita disposable income of Edmonton residents is one of the highest in the country."

Oddly, it makes no mention that Alberta also has the lowest minimum wage in Canada, $5.00 an hour for adults. That translates into a pay of about $800 a month before taxes, not very much no matter how low the cost of living is. The province also has the lowest rate of unionization in Canada.

Alberta, to borrow the immortal words of Ontario's Premier Mike Harris, has been "open for business" for some time.

I'm singularly unimpressed with the huddle of tall buildings—offices and headquarters of companies—that make up the business section of downtown. I wonder about our need to spike the skyline with concrete towers; I think maybe tall buildings are to businessmen what fur coats are to mistresses.

I walk down Jasper Avenue towards 96th Street. According to the map I found at the hotel, the two intersect. Jasper looks as though it was created for an upscale tourism onslaught that never happened. It's a remarkably deserted avenue, in spite of a scattering of park benches and a wonderful view: I'm starting to wonder if the locals know something I don't.

Perhaps it's a hangover from Vancouver, but I'm feeling a bit prickly: my personal early-warning system has kicked in. There's not even much car traffic. I start walking faster, a big-city walk that declares to the unseen *Don't mess with me*.

It's with a bit of relief that I catch sight of a couple on one of the benches down the road. From a distance, they could be a husband and wife catching some fresh air. He's a middle-aged white guy, with thinning red hair; the lady is Native. But there's something about them, I don't know what, but they feel wrong. I keep my eyes straight ahead as I pass them.

"Pat! Pat! Pat!"

Nothing like hearing your name called in a place where no one knows you.

I turn back, and rising from the bench is Joan.

I first met her at the Parkdale drop-in where I used to work, in Toronto's west end. Joan ran with a tough crowd: drugs, alcohol, inhalants—whatever was available, or could be ripped off from the weak or the careless. She was still attractive, though you had to look hard for the beauty, almost erased by need and abuse.

Her body was a commodity, available for trade: a roof for the night, a bottle, pills. Repeated pregnancy was a natural consequence, and each episode led her into a delusional ritual. In High Park, up the street from the drop-in, is Grenadier Pond. Though it's not terribly clean or inviting, it held some mystery that seemed to attract Joan. She'd go there nightly, to drink from the pond in her own kind of ceremony, some kind of seeking, that jeopardized both her and the fetus she carried.

The system's answer was to commit her until the infant was born, and if it lived, take it away. Grounds for committal were valid: she often didn't admit to being pregnant, not to herself, not to others. Of course, once the child was delivered, so was she, back to the streets, back to the life.

I lost sight of her after I moved away from Parkdale. It's probably been six or eight years since I last saw her. I've wondered about her, of course, along with the others I left behind. Was she still alive? Did she have AIDS? And here she is, rushing towards me and sweeping me into a rough embrace, thrilled and blown away.

Her customer is looking distinctly uncomfortable, caught out. Joan's too excited to pick that up; she pulls me by the hand over to the bench.

"This is Pat, from Toronto," she tells him excitedly, beaming down at him before sitting. He mumbles something, staring at his shoes. For a minute, the three of us share this tiny island in a sea of emptiness, then he's up and moving quickly away.

"Stop," Joan cries. "You don't have to be afraid of Pat, it's Pat Capponi, from Toronto!"

Transaction interruptus.

He looks back over his shoulder, mutters something about having to catch a bus.

I don't know if I should feel guilty or glad about driving away the only customer on the street. What was she going to charge him? What was he willing to offer?

We light up cigarettes from my pack. She seems to experience only a moment's regret that he's gone.

It becomes clear in seconds that she's either delusional or stoned or both. She has a can of root beer, the kind with a big mug pictured on the front. She holds it out for me, pointing to the picture with the index finger of her other hand.

"Look, a whole mug for less than a dollar, a whole one! A mug can cost close to five bucks. But here it is, not even a buck, see?"

The eighth wonder of the world. All I can figure is that she's thinking of a pitcher of beer, confusing the two.

Physically, she doesn't look too bad. I've seen her a lot worse, with black eyes and busted-up face. Her clothes, too, are in fair shape.

"How're you doing, Joan? Are you living anywhere?"

She twists around, pointing to a low-slung building on the other side of the street. A Salvation Army shelter. Her body is vibrating. I remember that, how you could feel her physically even at a distance.

It's odd, the comings and goings of the mind. The flashes of memory and reason, overwhelmed by steadily encroaching drug-induced psychosis. I am able to make out that she travelled from Toronto to the Yukon, where her father still lives. Time has no meaning to her, so neither of us knows if she's been away for years or months. I've made appointments I have to keep, but I'm reluctant to leave her here. I try to tell her about some of her old friends I've run into in Toronto, how they miss her and wonder about her, but she's having difficulty staying tuned in to me. To make up for her lost income, I slip her a few bucks from the stash in my pocket, and she hugs me again in farewell.

Walking away feels like desertion.

In bare minutes, I'm at 96th Street—more people here, certainly more cars.

I like to walk, it's the best way to get to know a new place, to get the feel and tempo of the streets. But now I carry my own disturbance with me, and I find I'm moving faster, trying to outpace the mood.

Soon after it intersects with Jasper, 96th deteriorates noticeably. Walking north, it's difficult to remember the beauty of the valley, faced with boarded-up stores and the hole-in-the-wall bars that riddle the street, from which, even in late afternoon, men and women stagger into the street. Most have two visible signs out front. One advertises VLTS (Video Lottery Terminals). The other is a dramatic poster showing a knife in a circle with a bar slashed across it; there are apparently a lot of stabbings in the inner city. The tall buildings that make the Edmonton skyline can't be seen here; there is no evidence of prosperity or civic pride. It's a dry, dirty landscape, peppered with threat. It feels airless, as though nature itself has abandoned the street.

Less than a thirty-minute walk from the Valley, I approach the railway tracks that intersect 96th, going east and west. I've already passed a series of agencies and missions and one very popular liquor store. It's possible here to see, on the streets leading out of this hopeless strip, neatly laid out, family-occupied, small wooden houses. These are neighbourhoods, according to the locals, constructed fifty, sixty, even eighty years ago; they are occupied now by a mix of people who find the low rents (due to the proximity to "skid row") appealing.

I briefly take a detour on these side streets—healthy-looking children play on trim lawns, watched over by one or another of their parents—till I stumble onto a truncated Chinatown, mostly mud and trucks at the moment, as road crews seem to be widening the street. I see a restaurant large enough, and busy enough, to suggest that it's probably not bad, but as I'm going in I notice a sign posted on the door: "We reserve the right to refuse service without explanation." This is certainly more direct than the dress-code warning that's usually posted in neighbourhoods that verge on poverty areas, or that are trendy enough to function even in the middle of drug or alcohol ghettoes. Those signs simply say "Dress Code:" the people they are intended for know what they mean.

A few blocks later I double back to the wasteland.

I pass by open fields just before the tracks that delineate the border of tolerance for street people. Here, you might think you were passing through a war zone during a momentary pause in the fighting. People—a mix of Native and white, men and women—lie collapsed in heaps of legs, arms and torsos, as though they've been mown down by gunfire.

I'm called out to (I am frequently mistaken for Native), waved at, encouraged to join the groups. But I see the empty bottles lying around, others still being emptied. Self-preservation rules. I simply wave back, and keep walking.

I VISIT THE BISSELL CENTRE, an agency supported by a mix of government, foundation and church funding. Here a dozen or so of those cut off from social assistance, for infractions large and small, while away their time in the basement drop-in drinking coffee, or listlessly playing cards, trying to appease hungry, rumbling stomachs. Night for them means crashing in abandoned buildings, or sleeping—at least till winter—out in the fields.

A study done in 1996 by the Edmonton Social Planning Council and the Edmonton Gleaners' Association, called "Two Paycheques Away: Social Policy and Hunger in Edmonton," concludes:

> [Of those using the food bank who were or are on welfare] a total of 34.1 per cent were allegedly cut off for "noncompliance," which [welfare] claims is due to not fulfilling a request from their social worker. Another one-third were supposedly cut off for "non-reporting," which is not providing information requested by the social worker.
>
> Further examination reveals a tendency for many [welfare] decisions to be trivial or insensitive to family crisis and other situations. For example, one unattached male reported being told by his social worker to cut his hair or be cut off for "noncompliance."

I meet the Reverend Faith Brace of the Inner City Pastoral Ministry in the Bissell drop-in. She's an unusual woman, and she has worked in the area for five years: listening, talking, serving hot lunches on Sundays, trying to bring a little humanity back into people's lives.

With Michael Walters from Our Voice—a spare-change magazine flogged by street vendors who prefer entrepreneurship to panhandling—she has edited two books of poetry, Songs of the Street, I and II. It's the poetry of self-expression, the sounds and songs of the lost and the broken. Vendors can buy them at cost, two dollars apiece, and sell them for five dollars, as they sell their magazines. It puts money directly into the pockets of the most needy, as well as enabling the voices of the powerless and forgotten to be heard.

I ask Faith about all the small churches I've seen nearby. I think I've counted thirteen or so, and she laughs and tells me she's heard that Edmonton is in either *Ripley's Believe It or Not* or *The Guinness Book of World Records* for the most churches in the smallest area. Lutheran, Baptist, Anglican, Catholic— every flavour. Most of their congregations no longer live in the area, having abandoned the inner city for the suburbs, but they still drive in on Sundays for the services. A lot of the work that goes on in "skid row" is funded by loose coalitions among the churches.

When I tell Faith about Joan, she tells me that 60 to 70 percent of the population of the inner city is Native. A number of these suffer in varying degrees from racism, poverty, lack of education and mental health and addiction problems. On the other hand, she says, Edmonton is the only city in

Canada where poor women get the best view: whether they look east or west, they can gaze out at either the river or the valley.

A fifty-two–bed women's residence is run from a renovated flatiron building behind the Salvation Army shelter where Joan is staying. Native women run the place, which was purchased by a church group and receives ongoing funding from various levels of government.

Faith likes how the women are treated there. "I like how they treat me, too. It's nice to be made welcome. Women who may never have encountered kindness in their lives find it there."

Ninety-sixth Street has its share of agencies and drop-ins, and its share of workers. I talk with one support worker who will have been in the area four years at the end of August. She asks that I not use her real name, so that she can speak freely. She grew up in a family where both parents were alcoholics, where sexual abuse started when she was eight. "Janet" told her mother, and was ordered not to speak about her father that way.

"I disappeared. Numbed out emotionally, tried to be the perfect child. I never quite made it, of course."

She left home at eighteen, married at nineteen, slowly but surely recreating the environment she thought she'd escaped.

Once she'd believed, coming out of poverty, that money would make her happy. Twelve years later, an alcoholic herself—

albeit a high-functioning one—she packed her two kids in the good car and left, spurred on by the fact that her four-year-old son, that same morning, had blown up her world by telling her that his daddy was playing with him sexually.

She knew if he came home before she got out, he'd convince her to stay; she knew she wasn't strong enough to resist him. She had two dollars in her pocket, but her chief motivation was the safety of her kids, and she was dogged by the frightening sense that her recreation of the past was getting too accurate.

The next day, the boy and his eight-year-old sister were videotaped by Children's Aid workers, and, through the use of dolls, both described episodes of sexual abuse. She eventually went to trial, and the abuser was convicted.

She has been sober for eight years now. Her kids have undergone tons of counselling.

"I was luckier than a lot of people, I could find out about resources and access them. I got that part of me from my mother. She was a very articulate woman to whom language was very important."

"Janet" was able to keep her kids fed most of the time, although 48 percent of her income from social services went to rent. The first time she used a food bank was at the agency where she now works.

"I was giving myself all the old messages, how inadequate I was. I was ashamed, nervous about coming down to the area.

This was skid row. It had this reputation: walk down the street and you get murdered."

The kids got used to eating lots of hamburger, hot dogs, macaroni, even, on lean days, sandwiches made with ketchup or sugar or bananas. Not understanding their new circumstances, they thought she was just "too cheap" when it came to buying clothing that would allow them to fit in at school. It was depressing; she knew it affected how they felt about themselves.

"I knew I had to get off social assistance, go back to school."

And she did, studying social work, which is how she ended up on staff at the Centre.

On the other side of the street is a liquor store. I tell her I watched as a small group of men and women tried to pool their diminished resources, searching their pockets and laboriously counting sums.

"I don't feel sorry for them. I know they could change if they wanted too, but it's tough. They come out of backgrounds of poverty and abuse. That gets no attention. Only the drinking."

Her children?

Her daughter is struggling with her past. She is currently on social assistance. Her son, diagnosed with Attention Deficit Disorder, still lives at home. He is a Cadet, which doesn't thrill her, but it seems to work for him. At least he sticks with it.

THE NEXT EVENING, I attend an orientation session for Meet the Street '98, a fund- and consciousness-raising event held annually at The Mustard Seed, a church-based community centre that houses a food bank as well as offering advocacy and outreach services. The building itself is very odd from the out-side—like an old car covered with primer paint, sagging a bit under the weight of age—and it has a checkered history.

Located towards the northern end of 96th, it began life as the First German Baptist Church; then, during World War II, it became Central Baptist. The congregation, uncomfortable in the steadily deteriorating neighbourhood, moved out in 1973 to new digs right across the river. For a while the church became a Chinese restaurant and bar, rumoured to be a good place to buy and sell dope. Then, right after the Urban Cow-boy trend, it became a country and western bar.

Now, with some funding from Corrections Canada, pri-vate donations and other grants, people here work with a vari-ety of individuals, including prisoners released from the feder-al system into Edmonton's core. Neil Maclean, who, like Faith Brace, is a chaplain, describes his work as rebuilding and investing in the lives of others.

All the staff do constant security checks of the building to ensure safety. "We have some rather interesting characters around here," Neil tells me, referring to the street addicts.

This is not a place where people are judged. At the begin-ning of March, Neil's own cousin died of an overdose of cocaine and heroin. He was a bright, good-looking kid. He'd had everything to live for, but got caught up; it took four days for his body to be found.

There's a picture over the stage, the stage that has replaced the altar: one white-robed arm, with a hand, palm up, just touching another hand, covered in cut-off gloves. Its pious charity bothers me, but I shrug it off.

The open hall is filling up with university-age students, workers and members of the activist community who've come, in the words of Faith, who's also here, to show solidarity with the people of the street. They will spend the night walking around the neighbourhood, in groups of three, getting a taste of what it's like to have nowhere to lay your head.

People are getting their marching orders from the organizers. They are put on the honour system and told not to spend more than three dollars, not to all go in one direction, not to spend the night in doughnut shops, and not to clump up in groups of more than three. Twenty teams are going out.

A young Asian police officer takes the podium and delivers some street advice to the nervous audience. He tells them not to interfere if they see something suspicious going on. He asks them to keep their identity markers clearly visible. He expects them to understand that police are necessarily rougher in this area than where they might be living. If the police approach them, they should be cooperative. People down here carry drugs and weapons, and the officers have to be more careful. "It's just like you see on that program 'Cops,'" he adds, drawing a laugh. He tells them that they will see prostitutes, druggies and sniffers, these last being the most unpredictable. Some of these guys won't hesitate to pull a knife, he warns; others might have TB or HIV/AIDS.

He reminds the audience that we're now coming to the end of the week in which the cheques are delivered, which means the partying has died down and the longer weeks of hunger and thirst are starting.

When he finishes, there is a yellow sheet distributed that defines the boundaries of Meet the Street '98, as well as a map with points of interest listed separately in some detail.

Having heard so much about the river valley and its beauty as a tourist spot, it's jarring to read at the top of the list: "Riverbank (North Saskatchewan River): Please do not go into the river valley. It is estimated over 250 homeless people sleep along the riverbank during the warmer months (April to October)."

Each person is also equipped with an identity to assume for the night, at least in his or her own mind; the details are typed out on a sheet. For instance, one "street person profile" reads:

Bernice
Sex: Female
Age: 52 years
Height: 5'6"
Weight: 150 lbs.

Hair: Brown

Appearance: Grey, scraggly, shoulder-length hair, wears a torn-up red winter coat year round and never washes her clothes. She speaks softly only when spoken to and often not about the subject. Arthritis has partially crippled her hands.

Bernice grew up on a farm east of Red Deer and only completed Grade 6 in school. She then had to stay home and care for her four younger brothers because her mom became very ill and her father was occupied running the farm. Bernice's mom died shortly afterwards and her father began to drink heavily. One night, her father went on a drunk and rolled his truck in the ditch. He suffered paralysis and brain damage. Child Welfare took Bernice and her four brothers into foster care. Bernice was separated from her brothers and never saw them again. Another farming family north of Lethbridge adopted her. Her only possession besides her clothing was a black and white picture of her family.

During her stay with this family, she began to suffer great depression and would often walk alone down the back country roads. Sometimes she would not come home for days and, when she did, she would receive a spanking from her adoptive father. Bernice was sent to school but never did complete any courses. Finally her new family, not knowing what to do for the girl, requested that Child Welfare take her back with the hopes of seeing her receive treatment they themselves could not offer.

Bernice was sent to an Alberta hospital. At 25, she was released to a rooming house in Edmonton where she received occasional visits from a social worker. One day, Bernice left the house, taking only a few clothes and the family picture. Since then she has wandered through the streets of Edmonton and Calgary, sometimes sleeping in the drop-in centre, but usually in an abandoned shed in Vic Park.

This night she discovers her shed is boarded up more securely and there is a man who scares her at the drop-in centre, so she has decided to wait out the night.

THE TEAMS ARE WISHED good luck, and told to return for breakfast and debriefing at about 6:00 a.m.

So, when the 4:00 a.m. wake-up call rattles me out of my sleep on my last day in Edmonton I curse and groan, but I'm there at 5:45 for the debriefing.

The building is already filled. Apparently people wandered back much earlier than they were supposed to, and most have already spoken about how they spent their night. People got really bored. Apparently the viewing/experiencing wasn't good tonight; the denizens of the street weren't in evidence. Motivated by lack of sleep and subsequent empathetic meltdown, I call out that they must have all gone to the suburbs and were spending the night pretending they were homeowners.

We eat breakfast, while some people bring out decks of cards, and others just chat quietly. Apparently, two to three thousand folks have done the same thing all across Canada, trying to learn and understand what it's like to be homeless and friendless.

Even though it didn't work out so well here tonight, from the point of view of the street people, it was still an honest and valuable attempt to experience a night without the comforts of a television and a couch, a flush toilet and a fridge, or even a safe place to sit. The passport for Meet the Street '98 has some interesting questions for people to consider, within the roles they've been assigned:

- Is there a place you would feel safe sleeping?
- Who could you call for help?
- Who cares about you?
- Who would want to hurt you?
- Who is in charge of your life?

The name of this place, The Mustard Seed, comes from a biblical quotation: with the faith equivalent to a grain of mustard seed, one can move mountains.

And they need to.

"IF YOU BELIEVE IN basic, fundamental values, this is a hard, dry, angry place to be." So says Brian Bechtel of the Edmonton Social Planning Council. He is noticeably despairing of the attitude of the government, and the new tenor of public discussion: you get shouted down. Speak up, speak out, and you'll be attacked, personally, in the media.

"There's never any real public consternation about the things the government's doing. No political diversity in this province. We only change governments every forty years." He's watched the virtual destruction of public advocacy. "So many groups once supported by government are gone. If they could put us out of business, they would."

With increasing numbers of people thrown off welfare, and with drastic cutbacks to social spending, the pressure and the difficulties continue to rise. Over two thousand people a year are cut from Alberta's welfare rolls, now that (as stated in the September 1, 1997 issue of *Alberta Report*) welfare has become "work fare" in Alberta.

One person who found herself cut off for alleged infractions was a fifty-one-year-old woman, and mother of three,

Theresa Margaret McBryan. When that happened, she launched an appeal, which failed. What makes her different from so many others is that she was the first person to go on and fight the decision of the appeal body, the Citizens Appeal and Advisory Secretariat.

Quoting social services spokesman Bob Scott, *Alberta Report* claims that there are thirty-one welfare panels that hear about 2,500 appeals a year. Scott also goes on to declare: "The people appointed [to these panels] by the minister are first recommended by MLAs. They are not really political or partisan choices. In 77% of the cases, they uphold the [social services] department's decision."

In her sworn affidavit to the Court of Queen's Bench of Alberta, Theresa declares that she was advised, on February 17, 1997, that her social assistance funding was terminated by file closure on or about February 13, 1997, for alleged breach of Section 16 (2)(e) of the Social Development Act, for "refusing or neglecting to avail myself of appropriate training or rehabilitative measures."

She'd suffered an emotional breakdown, resulting from traumatic childhood sexual abuse, in 1983; at the time she was a single parent trying to raise three children, who are now twenty-two, twenty and eighteen. She was put on Assured Income for the Severely Handicapped (AISH). Most people on permanent disability pensions have a great, learned reluctance to jeopardize it by working or returning to school. The fear is, quite basically, that if, having given it up, a person gets sick again, it means life on the much smaller welfare income while trying to jump through the hoops of reapplying. It's the ultimate disincentive.

Theresa wanted to work, and to learn, so she gave up her assured income under AISH in order to attend Grant MacEwan Community College on a full-time basis, where she completed the Graphic Design and Illustration Program. After completing the course, she went back on social assistance while searching for a full-time job in the graphic design industry, or temporary and part-time positions in the retail field. She lived outside Edmonton in a town called Bon Accord. After her car died, she had to take the Greyhound, when she had bus fare, or hitchhike into the city when she didn't, for interviews and to submit job applications.

On October 30, 1996, she was referred to the Goodwill Rehabilitation Services of Alberta and their Power of Work program by her social assistance worker, and on December 2, 1996, she began attending the compulsory work-readiness classes. Then, perhaps as a consequence of living on a poverty diet of "tea and potatoes," she got sick. Her doctor told her to take ten days off, and she did, sending in her doctor's note.

It wasn't good enough for the system. Her income of $394 a month, already drastically reduced from the level of AISH, was cut off, which meant that she had to give up her apartment, and most of her furniture and possessions. She found

herself living in a friend's unheated garage, the only other
alternatives being a women's shelter or life on the street.

She has many supporters in her fight, including Pam Barrett, leader of the New Democrats in Alberta. In a press release
dated June 19, 1997, Barrett states:

> This Conservative government policy of systemat-
> ically denying benefits regardless of the economic
> circumstances of the persons involved results from
> the 1993 welfare reforms. Every month the govern-
> ment puts out a news release bragging about the
> reduction in the welfare caseload, failing to point
> out that this is being done at the expense of Alber-
> tans like Theresa McBryan. It is clear to me that
> this is one of the many cases where the govern-
> ment may be making itself look good by contra-
> vening its own Social Development Act. Since I
> opened my community office two months ago, my
> constituency staff have already dealt with 36 cases
> involving the denial of welfare benefits to people
> in need. Many of the cases involve single parents
> with young children. Inner city agencies and advo-
> cates for the poor are aware of hundreds of cases
> similar to the one that is giving rise to the court
> challenge. A major problem is that people involved
> with the social services system are afraid to come
> forward to expose the fundamental unfairness of

the Conservative government's policies. They feel vulnerable and fear being punished further.

Theresa herself says:

For this government so far the anti-poor stance has worked. Enough people have believed the fairy tale that it was money spent on social services that caused the deficit. Carrying around their maxed-out credit cards, dodging creditors with their display phones, people don't think too much. Every month the government proudly trots out more numbers about how many more people must be working now because they are not on welfare anymore. My supporters and I want to remind those who implement government policies that the statistics they release are first and always real people. Real people are paying with their health, their security, their happiness, their children's futures and in some cases with their very lives to be part of those happy numbers government functionaries release every month.

Theresa has sent me a whole information package. Included in it is a letter from Senator Erminie J. Cohen of New Brunswick, dated August 5, 1997, in which she declares on impressive Senate letterhead:

The poor are easy targets. In a society that no longer accepts racial intolerance, the poor are one of the few minorities we can still bash over the head. They suffer the indignity of poverty; is it any wonder they feel so helpless and abandoned! Where is the humanity that once served our welfare system so proudly? Are bureaucracy, efficiency and fiscal restraints still so necessary? Has anyone taken a good hard look at the implications of government policies and where it is taking us as a nation? This is not the kind of society that we want. We want a society that "once was"—when we not only provided for the poor, but were willing to do whatever was humanely possible to allow our neighbours to live in dignity and hope. A hand up—not a hand down! . . . This hardened attitude of governments to welfare recipients is challenging the face of Canada and what we value as Canadians. Bravo! Good luck! Do what you must do. You are a crusader and one whose time has come.

The judge at the Court of Queen's Bench ruled that the appeal panel didn't follow the correct procedure by failing to provide McBryan with proper reasons for denying her benefits. This required that a new appeal panel be struck, which it was—and, of course, that new panel upheld the department's original decision.

Theresa and her supporters will be back in court soon.

All this takes money, which requires fundraising, and the ability to communicate and understand, to attend meetings, to speak to media, to bare your life to strangers. This is extraordinarily difficult when your stomach is empty, your home reduced to a shack, when you are alienating the very system that you must depend on.

"Alberta is a very tiresome place," Theresa tells me. "The land is flat with square corners and straight roads. Its people are the same. Rigid, narrow-minded, in a sterile world."

Theresa is an articulate, motivated, intelligent woman. She doesn't fit the public notion of who a welfare recipient is. The fellow denied income and sleeping on the riverbank could never have garnered the support she has, would never have been able to jump through all the legal hoops, fill in and understand all the forms and jargon, even look sympathetic and clean in court.

Her fight is their fight, but it's unlikely that other dispossessed people will even hear about what she's undertaken. In their rooms without walls or ceilings or fridges or television or radios or phones, in their lives without purpose or comfort or human connections, nothing exists except the damp of the grass that serves as their bed, and the wrath of strangers who feel they've given too much.

If Theresa wins her protracted struggle, she personally will see $394 a month. But it might mean a lot more than that for the country that has called her "undeserving."

"The middle class doesn't want to know," Theresa says, "and the press doesn't want to tell them. Reports of inner-city kids going to school with no breakfast, with no lunch, no proper clothing in winter. Fifteen years from now when one of those kids points a gun in our face and orders us to empty the till, we'll catch on to the notion of consequences."

We talk again some months later.

"I think it's more disappointing for my backers than for me," she tells me. "You know, they expect a rational response to a rational argument. I've learned the hard way that that just doesn't happen."

The judge in the second court challenge ruled unequivocally against her.

"Luck of the draw, we got clobbered by a redneck judge."

Social services, politicians, agencies. She sighs deeply.

"There's something almost awful, almost disgustingly horrible about these people. Sometimes, watching them, it's like—I don't know—a peep show, indecent. The way they manoeuvre to protect themselves, to protect what they have."

The only positive for her personally, and it's a big one, is this:

"Win or lose, I come out of this a little stronger. Any tendency I might have had left to internalize the things they say about me totally dissipates when I see what idiots they are. I have an intact sense of self: I guess I was in the right place at the right time."

She points out that what they've spent on lawyers could have enabled them to pay out her stipend for ten years.

"People are very scared, terrified of stepping out of line, losing their place at the trough."

She expects there might be another appeal, but she has no idea where the money will come from. At this moment, she's not anxious to go back to court. She's living with her daughter and son-in-law, an arrangement that thrills none of them. And she's extremely reluctant to reapply to the system that discarded her.

Part of the Judge's decision reads as follows:

> Ms. McBryan also tried to frame the issue in terms of "bad attitude." That is also potentially misleading. Presumably if Ms. McBryan had done everything that was legitimately expected of her in the program, she would have been at complete liberty to criticize the program, the program deliverers, the cost of the program, etc., and to have attempted to get her fellow students, and the public, to rebel against the program.
>
> Although the finding against Ms. McBryan contained a comment by the panel that Ms. McBryan had an "unacceptable attitude toward

the intent behind the SFI program" a reading of
the Panel's decision in its entirety leads inex-
orably to the conclusion that the Panel supported the Director's decision because the Panel concluded, on the basis of the evidence that it heard,
that Ms. McBryan breached the program's com-
ponents and that these breaches were attributable
not to impossibility for medical reasons, or
impossibility for transportation reasons, but to a
lack of willingness on Ms. McBryan's part to
comply with the program, in other words, to her
poor attitude to the program.

The men and women slashed from the Supports for Independence rolls who are now sleeping in Edmonton's fields can
slumber on; they're in no danger of rescue.

In 1996, the number of unemployed in Alberta was
118,000. Youth unemployment was over 15 percent. In Edmonton, 155,00 residents live under the poverty line.

This is not Vancouver: no one here upholds the comfortable idea of providing a "living room" where people can while
away their lives; here the workers can only try—against great
odds—to keep people alive.

During the research and writing of this book, I have found
a new level of awareness in the leadership rising out of the
communities of the poor. In these places, an instant intimacy

is created by shared knowledge and a recognition of the realities of our times. Ultimately, we are in this by ourselves. We do the suffering, we are the ones who go hungry, or watch our children long for what other kids take for granted. We know the truth behind the current political rhetoric. We know how angry the middle-class communities around us get when the poor spill over to their sidewalks, or stand in the alcoves of their stores, or panhandle in front of their liquor outlets. We know that the solutions foisted on us haven't worked, and won't work. We even have ideas as to how they might be radically improved. But there is no one willing to listen.

Expertise doesn't come from a life lived. Apparently, it comes from textbook analysis in the safety of university classes; it comes from BAS and MAS and PHDS. And it comes without the understanding that our past and present system was inadequate and misdirected and hopelessly out of touch with everyday reality—except insofar as it mirrored and reinforced the hierarchy encountered daily by those who are driven to it.

We have a triage system in place that allows first entry to those least damaged and most capable of "appreciating" what they're given. People who might well have made it anyway swell our agency statistics, make good fundraising anecdotes, while those who have been rejected and abused almost since day one continue in downward, self-destructive spirals with no fear of interference in the form of intervention.

And it doesn't seem to matter which of the various helping systems is involved. They have more shared characteristics than their populations.

I'M KILLING TIME AT the Edmonton airport, waiting for a bar called Balloons to open. My flight's been delayed. I hate when that happens. My fear-of-flying tranquillizers lose their potency, having been exquisitely timed to be at full strength for the takeoff. Still, it gives me time to do what Sam, the cab driver who brought me here, suggested.

We'd been chatting during the drive, all the regular kinds of conversation you have in a taxi on the way to the airport. You know—where are you off to, where do you live, what were you doing here?

When I mention the bars on 96th Street and their VLTs, he shakes his head and starts telling me about his experiences with the slot machines. He'd been addicted to them, the same way people get addicted to booze or drugs. Wasted hundreds, maybe thousands of dollars. It's been a year and a half since he played them.

"How'd you beat it?"

"I have three brothers. We're all married, and my father really wanted to live long enough to see his first grandchild. My brothers married women who didn't really want children, so I felt it was up to me.

"My wife refused to get pregnant as long as I was throwing money away on those machines. I quit cold turkey. Two months later she announced she was pregnant."

He glances back at me, wondering if I'll laugh at him.

"I've got to tell you, I'm not a fanatic or anything, but I'm sure God had a hand in this. The baby was born premature at six months. The next three months I concentrated so hard on him, prayed and stayed so focused on him, the thought of playing the slots never came up."

The boy is fine now, the pride of his parents, the joy of his grandfather.

He tells me other drivers at his company didn't fare as well. It got so bad that they'd pick up a fare and as soon as they'd dropped him off, they'd take the money down to the nearest VLT. The company instituted new rules: any driver whose cab was seen parked in front of one of those places, any driver who didn't respond to the dispatcher when on duty, was automatically fired.

"So tell me, what's the lure?"

He laughed. "There's a bar in the airport that has a few machines. Check it out yourself, but be careful."

While I'd been in Vancouver, I'd visited the casino in the basement of the hotel I was staying in. I'd never gone to it the other half-dozen times I'd stayed there. I half suspected there would be a dress code, but one of the hotel staff reassured me that there wasn't.

I took forty dollars out of the stash of cash I had to carry, not having credit cards or sufficient, acceptable identification to cash travellers' cheques.

My first thought was that there were more staff than players, and that the staff were better dressed. The place had a desultory feel about it, as though someone had decided to throw the bash of the year and only a handful of people showed up. I asked one of the security people about this. He laughed and told me that part of the problem was that they were set up for VLTs, but they had not been allowed in yet. They had poker, and roulette, where I lost half of the money I'd allocated. But there was no excitement, no glamour, no lure. I shrugged and walked away, figuring maybe the gambling issue was overstated.

This bar, Balloons, has one of those metal security fences, and a staff member is starting to push it back. I'm right there, but already two of three machines are occupied, two gentlemen sitting on the high stools, looking like they've been there all their lives. Both are smoking.

I take the third stool and stare uneasily at this VLT, waiting for it to bite.

It takes paper money, and I feed it a five-dollar bill. It's like a particularly costly computer game. Lights, action: you don't even have to pull down the arm or do anything particularly strenuous—just press spin and you're off. It's not relaxing; it's not boring. Seems like no time at all till it's eating another five bucks.

Maybe just once more.

I'm talking to myself: I won't be getting this back, the machine doesn't give receipts. And there's a danger of winning, and if I win, I know my plane will crash. Life is like that. I start sweating, wanting to use up the credits left and get out of there.

One of the men beside me asks the other what time it is.

He says, in a deadened voice, "Christ, I don't know."

They laugh, both of them, not a nice laugh, not a cheerful laugh, knowing what's important—and it isn't time or destinations.

It's with great relief that I use the last of the credit left on my machine and get the hell out of there.

Maybe I was just spooked by my cab driver, I think, once I'm safely aloft. It's just a stupid machine, after all. Nonetheless, I have the strangest sense of having narrowly escaped a very bad thing.

CHAPTER THREE

WINNIPEG

PAULINE'S HOUSE IS ONE of the oddest I've ever been in. Small to begin with, it's been divided lengthwise into two separate households, and it has the straight-ahead feel of a trailer. The front entrance, on Stella Avenue, is blocked off; access to her place is through the back laneway, while a side entrance serves the residents of the other half. There are five houses, owned by the same landlord, carved up in similar fashion.

The lock on the back door is inadequate at best. Pauline puts more faith in a large padlock, but it has only one key, so "security" is sacrificed to permit me to come and go as I please.

I've been given my own room. Closest to the kitchen, it's off the hallway that leads into the living room, attractive and comfortable, behind which is Pauline's bedroom.

I have a narrow bed, and beside it, resting on a milk crate, is a reading lamp which I fear she's taken from her own bedroom. There is also a desk I could use if I were used to working at one.

The bathroom off the kitchen has a noisy fan in place of a window, and when I go in there, I assume it has been left on. When it abruptly ceases its racket as I'm preparing for a shower, I realize that the tenant on the other side of the house has just turned his off.

Pauline's is the only one of these houses with a small, fenced-in garden; everyone else has to settle for driveways of pebbles and dust. She gets help with plants and insects and advice about soil from two aboriginal women, both community workers, who share a house nearby and lean companionably over the fence. That they wish they had their own garden is very evident.

There are two kids chasing each other around a shed out back. The youngest boy lives with his grandmother and likes to introduce himself by saying, "My mummy killed a guy."

Pauline finds it funny that she represents an island of stability to her friends, the most grown-up and settled person they know.

I first met Pauline a year ago. I'd been invited to give the keynote speech at a conference called Stirring Up a Storm: Feminist Activism across Communities and Universities, held at the University of Winnipeg. Pauline had been given the task of introducing me on the night of my speech, and we also served on a panel together the following afternoon. Through Pauline and her network, I was able to see and understand more about Winnipeg than I could by looking out my window at the Fort Garry Hotel, where I'd been booked.

She will be fifty-three this year. Born in Yorkshire, she has lived in Winnipeg since 1981.

"I've always thought of my father as the last serf," she laughs. He was a farm worker, and they'd move to different areas of Yorkshire every two years. In exchange for his labour, they'd be given a place to live, food and some money. She got called "stupid" a lot, in school and by her verbally and physically abusive mother.

"School was harsh, with the strap and caning, blackboard erasers flying through the air. My first take-home reports from new schools would always say: 'Pauline could do better if she tried.' 'Uncooperative' was usually written in, too."

Her father never did anything to temper his wife's behaviour. "She had aspirations above her station, which caused her to live in a delusionary kind of world. She was a royalist, and sometimes, in exasperation, I'd tell her, 'In the old days, you'd have been a scullery maid in the castle.'"

Pauline understood the class system from a very early age.

She'd watch the relationship between her father and his bosses. "He wouldn't tug at his forelock, but there was a kind of cap-in-hand subservience."

Her mother, on the other hand, would move into a new place, strip it down, paper and paint and dig a garden. She also dressed very differently from the other farmhands' wives, in a distinctly middle-class look. "My mother made her own clothes with a style the other women didn't seem to have, topped off by the ever present purse and gloves, like the Queen herself. In the country, it was oddly out of place."

Pauline left home for the first time at the age of fifteen. She lived in a rented trailer down by the railway tracks and worked part-time at the cosmetic counter in Woolworth's. Never encouraged to go on with school, she finished at age sixteen.

"My mother died in 1980 from cancer. She was so angry, so bitter. Same dying as she was living. She hadn't gotten what she wanted from life. The best gift she ever gave me was to serve as a warning—not to repeat her mistakes."

Pauline took up with a young man who worked as a clerk in the Royal Air Force. Wanting a proper home, a family that was loving, and safety and security, she married in 1964. "It was all illusion," she says sadly.

He left the RAF, and both of them started working in a succession of bars and hotels. He was a drinker. And soon she started, too. "It wasn't until after I left him that I realized I had a drinking problem. I couldn't even fall asleep without it."

They had two sons, but her husband was abusive. It got so bad that she fantasized about killing him.

"I'd imagine I stuck a knife in his heart, turned it round and round and watch the fucker die. I had wallpaper in my kitchen with designs all over it. I would count those designs while he bitched at me.

"One day, at work in the catering kitchen, he was standing there, his mouth going. I couldn't hear a thing he was saying, but I'd had it. I walk towards him, slowly, with a knife pointed at him. Just then, a friend walked in, shouted at me and quite gently took the knife out of my hand."

She still shudders to think about it. "I could have done it. I could have gone to jail. It's really bizarre to know how ugly you can become. To actually want to take another person's life." She had been so ground down, she'd internalized all the messages first from her mother and then from her husband: *You're so fucking useless. This is good enough for you. Who do you think you are, you uppity cow?*

She left that same day, and never went back.

Her friend and sometime saviour, Ron, picked up the kids from school and loaded her possessions into his car. Within a month, she'd found a job and a place to live. When her husband tried to force her back, Ron gave him a beating. He continued to harass her for two years, with phone calls and suicide threats.

Her two boys, eleven and nine, were angry with her at first

for leaving their dad. Even though they'd grown up witnessing physical violence between their warring parents, it was a case of "the devil you know." It took two months before they started to relax and enjoy the new arrangement. She, meanwhile, worked at a variety of jobs, managing a shoe store for a time, then working on the buses as a conductor. Her kids would come home from school and be on their own, latchkey kids. Pauline felt like a hamster in a cage going round and round. Only surviving.

Her parents and sister had emigrated to Canada, and when her mother was diagnosed with cancer, her father sent her the airfare for her and the boys to come as well. She needed her ex's permission to take the children out of England.

"The only leverage I had was the outstanding support payments. I could have had him sent to jail." Still, he managed to persuade the younger boy to stay with him. She remembers her son crying, and explaining to her that he couldn't leave, because if he did he'd never see his dad again. "I didn't play that game with him. You know, 'If you stay, you might never see *me* again.' But it was really harsh. My oldest boy viewed his brother as a traitor, even refusing to speak to him, while I felt like I'd abandoned him."

She's asked him about it in the last few years. "That was the first adult decision I ever made in my life," he tells her, refusing her offer of guilt. And the two brothers are back on speaking terms.

In Canada, she lived for a time with her dad in a one-bedroom on Portage Avenue. Within a month she had a job at Eaton's.

"I used to wonder where all the people were. In London, there were people everywhere, any time of day or night. Here, even on the buses, people would move away from any contact with each other."

She worked on getting rid of her drinking problem. "I knew I could be a pretty ugly drunk. I used to fight physically if I wasn't surrounded by good friends, if someone pressed the right triggers." She struggled with depression and alienation, weighed down by a lifetime of only surviving.

Her sister tried to help. Pauline and her son moved in with her, and Margo, involved with community theatre, introduced Pauline to her wide circle of friends. "I still had no sense of my own worth," Pauline remembers. "I would find myself in rooms full of people, all talking, and I was no longer myself, just Margo's sister."

She pulled herself out of the depths and went after a future. With government assistance, she went full-time to Red River Community College. She volunteered on a twenty-four-hour crisis line, after ten weeks of training. "I'd already lived what many of the callers were going through, but now I was learning to see it differently. I enjoyed it, because I felt useful. It became part of my own healing."

She did a six-month placement at the Community

Unemployment Help Centre, working the front desk, learning how to read UIC rules and regulations.

"I became a counsellor and an advocate, and even started acting in community theatre: No Frills theatrics. After four years at the Help Centre, I moved on to work as a publicist for the Popular Theatre Alliance. I learned about community organizing and the media."

Pauline started freelancing, working with community groups. But hard times were coming—not just for her, but for the whole province. She'd never had difficulty finding a job, not in fifteen years. They weren't great jobs, most of them, but they'd paid the bills and bought the groceries. Now, government cuts either forced the closure of the groups she worked with, or left them with so little that there was no option of paid work. She found herself with no savings and no UI entitlement. She was forced on to welfare. It was shocking, how quickly she became demoralized, ashamed that she didn't have a job.

"You get disconnected from the loop. Nobody knows you, job contacts dry up, networks disappear. I hid away here. My rent was $240, and welfare was about $277." The most she'd ever made in her life was $24,000 one year. "It wasn't so much the money. People, my friends, would feed me. Even my land-lord was patient. It was that scrapheap kind of feeling. No longer employable, no longer useful."

It seemed a natural fit, then, to apply for and win the job of provincial coordinator for the Manitoba Action Committee on the Status of Women, a grand title for what was essentially a part-time job. But that job, too, was dependent on government grants, and now Pauline is on Employment Insurance, which will run out in November.

Now that she's over fifty, she worries a little about aging, and she's still coming to terms with her body's middle-aged changes: the stomach that's no longer quite as flat, the overwhelming fatigue that sets in after late nights and early mornings. She worries, too, about the future, what she'll do without a pension. She's lived long with poverty and knows its toll. And by the time she's too old to fend for herself, she's pretty sure that our attitude to the poor and elderly will have gotten even worse. This is one of the reasons why she values community and friends.

So, she's decided to do the ultimate in job searches: she's running for city council.

IT IS POSSIBLE TO DRIVE from one end of Winnipeg to the other in thirty minutes. The city has a population of under 700,000 people. And judging by the annoying television commercial that seems to be airing every time I switch to the TV-listings channel, you'd suspect that many of those 700,000 are less than stellar citizens. The commercial begins with an angelic child musing aloud about right and wrong. A voiceover in the key of dominant male authority goes something like this:

"Your children learn morality from you. Set a good example. Stealing cable is wrong."

A bus shelter sports a huge, dramatically black-and-white ad: the left side—in bold, biblical script—declares "Thou Shalt Not Steal;" the right side advertises Loss Prevention Seminars. The same ad looms from billboards around the city. Theft seems to be the only growth industry here. I start to feel as though I'm in one of those discount stores in a bad neighbourhood, the kind that don't welcome so much as caution: *No credit, shoplifters will be prosecuted, all parcels and bags must be left at the counter, no pets, no food, no smoking, no exchanges, all sales are final.*

There is an ugly, oppressive feeling here.

I watch a local cable show where an enthusiastic interviewer stops people on the street, asking them the "Question of the Day": "What attracts you to downtown?"

In spite of her upbeat effort, nobody answers the question as posed. Instead, people talk about fears for their safety, or their preference for the relative security of suburban malls.

Pauline offers to show me around. I meet her at her former office and we walk to her favourite restaurant, a grimy diner with working jukeboxes at every booth. On Selkirk, once referred to as "the jewel of the North End," it's practically the only business on the block that's still functioning. Other storefronts are closed or abandoned, as if they've fallen victim to a widespread poverty plague. The food here is cheap and unhealthy, just the way I like it, and you can smoke anywhere.

I'm already starting to feel more at home when an old woman ambles in and up to our booth to look for the denture she'd put aside to eat lunch and forgotten to pop back in. Obligingly, we all stand up and search behind the cushions and the sugar dispenser, but it's likely gone into the garbage with the scraps, and a tired waitress leads her into the back to search through the leftovers and dirty napkins.

The rest of the afternoon becomes a blur of inner-city misery.

Pauline has found a friend who has a car and drives, and so we tour the communities edging the downtown. I find a concentration of rooming and boarding houses in "murder row," which boarders the "granola belt," where artists and young professionals live, nervously but cheaply. Block after block of boarded-up stores. Empty social housing units where not even the desperate poor want to live. Pauline shows me the parks where the children of the poor congregate in gangs, united by deprivation and an awareness that they've already been dealt out of the game.

Later, I'm introduced to a photographer who recently lost her job through downsizing. She and her partner live in an area of high crime, and it was getting so bad that she felt she had to make some effort to reduce their fear and anxiety levels. She started going into the park bordering their house, where the kid gangs flourish, bringing her camera with her.

It took some time, but gradually the children stood still

long enough to have their photos taken. The results are stacked in a pile between us, black-and-white indictments of the city, in eight-year-old faces with ninety-year-old eyes. It's very hard to look into those eyes.

"Some of them had never seen a picture of themselves," the photographer says, shaking her head.

In groups and singly, the kids flash gang signs. Everyone wears the same brand of new running shoes, perhaps from an "interrupted" shipment, and the same defiant stare. Most look painfully undernourished.

The only positive to be found is in the gang groupings: a multiracial composition of white, Native, Asian and black. An acknowledgment of the central unifying fact of shared hardship, abuse and neglect.

My walk this afternoon takes me downtown via Main Street. Getting there takes me past the lost and the broken and the occasional predator.

Winnipeg's downtown is at best uninspiring. A lot of money is being expended on a showcase community centre for Natives that will impress the hell out of the tourists. But, like the painted buffalo on the grey cement of the nearby overpass on Main Street, snorting carbon monoxide fumes from the cars and trucks edging past the construction, Winnipeg prefers to see its aboriginal population through the glory of their past, ignoring the present-day misery of the community, mostly north of Main. Winnipeg will be hosting the Pan American summer games in 1999, and that has provided the impetus, the excuse, for the clean-up now underway. The city is trying to buy up a couple of the most disreputable hotels, which resemble the SROs in Vancouver and are often hotbeds of criminal activity, including the sale and consumption of drugs, prostitution and the fencing of stolen goods.

The Portage Village Inn at Portage Avenue and Donald Street, a den for drug dealers, drunks and thieves, will soon be out of business. The city expects to close a deal next week to buy the hotel for about $400,000. The property's value has been assessed at $350,000. The sole purpose is to close the business and force its clientele to move elsewhere, said Councillor Mike O'Shaughnessy (Old Kildonan), chairman of the city's property and development committee.

Fear of crime has been a major barrier to efforts to draw more people downtown and the Portage Village Inn was one of the most visible manifestations of the problem. However, the [Inn's] owner questioned whether closing [the hotel and bar] would clean up the mess in the downtown.

'There are a lot of glue-sniffing, Lysol-drinking, dope-smoking rubbies in this town who like to lie

down on the sidewalk and sleep,' Chuck Green
said. 'They're just shifting the problem from one
area to another, they're not eliminating it.'
                                    —*David O'Brien,*
                    Winnipeg Free Press, June 18, 1998

Pauline tells me that little of the "sprucing up, covering
up" money is making it north of Main.

Lately, the city newspapers have been poking front-page
fun at the council's efforts to silence their own "bug doctor,"
whom reporters were frequently wont to call with questions
about mosquitoes. They are particularly bad this year—too
much rain followed by too much heat, making for breeding
heaven. I suppose he was a bit too forthcoming, because now
he doesn't take their calls. It's the way cities handle a great
many of their problems: by pretending they don't exist.

PEOPLE KEEP TELLING ME—mind you, not poor people—how
wonderful Winnipeg is in the summer. About the beautiful
beaches and parks. What a large cultural community it has,
with art and music festivals and celebrations. *Toronto Star*
restaurant critic Cynthia Wine, who was brought up in Winnipeg's north-end suburbs and lived in the city as a young
adult in the late 1960s and early '70s, explains that people's
perspective on the city depends on which ghetto they're in.

Cynthia now lives in Toronto, and after my first visit to Winnipeg I talked to her about her hometown. I told her that I had the feeling that the people I ran into there, mostly employed in good jobs or pursuing arts careers, who kept insisting that Winnipeg was a wonderful place to live, were lying through their teeth. Maybe more to themselves than to me.

"I can understand that the Winnipeg I remember could seem cold and austere to anyone seeing it for the first time. Everything that's good about it is hidden indoors, in private homes—that's where it all happens, all the socializing, all the warmth of friends and family. If you're young, you'd hang out downtown, that being the space between The Bay and Eaton's, but being a grown-up, being married, meant all the socializing was done at home. When I moved to Toronto, I found it a bit of a shock that there's quite a different weight put on, a heavier significance it never had in Winnipeg, to 'having people over.'

"I was a single parent; sometimes I wouldn't be able to get a babysitter, and I'd say to a guy who wanted to go out with me, 'Come on over, we'll have supper and watch television,' and he'd be standing there, shifting uncomfortably from one foot to another, not knowing what to do with himself. It's not done in Toronto. If you want to get together, you meet at the Second Cup or Starbucks or a restaurant."

Her parents were immigrants, and the early years were not cushioned by wealth. But there were lots of other immigrants, and that was part of what made the community lively and close.

"All the stories that would be told, all around overcoming obstacles and hardships, funny and sad and heroic stories. Poverty was such a large part of the backdrop, a shared experience that created common bonds."

Cynthia still remembers the usual, but nonetheless painful, anti-Semitic taunts of the children—prejudices learned, no doubt, from their parents. And the beaches I'd heard so much about?

"Beautiful beaches, just an hour's drive from the city. Winnipeg Beach, Victoria Beach. Actually, I remember when there where signs posted there, 'No Dogs, No Jews allowed.' And the Forks, where the Red River and the Assinaboine meet, is quite wonderful."

When I ask if there was a large Native presence in the downtown back then, she thinks for a moment.

"Yes. Not as bedraggled and despairing as it is now, but yes. Nastier people used to call the downtown 'Moccasin Square Gardens.' There was drinking and poverty. And no one else in Winnipeg ever ate or drank outside. It was always peculiar like that, overly fastidious and health-conscious. In fact, for a long time it was against the law for restaurants to have outside dining available. I keep hearing from my family back home how exciting it is now that Corydon Avenue—in about a two-block area—actually has Italian restaurants with outdoor patios. That probably really set the Natives apart, this outside living in a city where no one spent real time outside.

"I guess what I love about Winnipeg is the openness, the big open sky, the white, wooden houses set far apart, and everyone has a garden: a symbol of the struggle against the elements, the determination to overcome the harsh climate and create life."

A FEW DAYS LATER, Freda bustles in with her two boys, one a toddler, the other a bright, active four-year-old. She'd accepted my offer of a cab ride down to Pauline's house. Pauline has offered to play outside with the kids while we speak. She knows Freda through her theatre activities.

After doling out bologna-and-cheese sandwiches to the kids for a "picnic lunch," she sighs, pours herself a cup of coffee and sits down at the kitchen table to roll a joint.

"I can't get through the morning without my first joint and my coffee," she says, inhaling contentedly.

She's thirty-four years old. Her mother gave birth to her in a hospital, the only one in the area where she lived, about fifty kilometres from the Pine Creek reserve, an eight-hour drive north of Winnipeg. Although there are more people living there now, at the time there were only a few thousand inhabitants. With world-weary cynicism, she adds: "Old men are still molesting children, granddaughters still having grandfathers' kids."

She calls her mother a whore, and initially I assume she means it in a professional sense, but she clarifies: "Mom had twelve kids by five different fathers. She palmed most of us off on her mother."

The reserve had electricity but no running water. And no central dump. Waste was collected in slop pails that were emptied in the bush. Water came from little dugouts by the dirt road leading into the reserve.

Freda remembers her grandmother sending her out with the other children on weekends to collect beer bottles in empty potato sacks. They'd range from one end of the reserve to the other collecting their treasure.

"Money was scarce. We ate anything that walked, except dogs."

She felt secure with her grandmother, loved and happy. Those were the best years of her life. Even counting the time when, while collecting chokecherries, she suffered a nasty cut on her foot from a rusty tin can thrown with other garbage into the bush. Her foot took six months to heal, and she still requires physiotherapy.

"My grandmother gave me wisdom. She taught me how to cook, to clean."

It all fell apart when her mother came to collect her and take her off the reserve. She had taken up with a white cab driver, an "Irish man from Ireland" named Fred.

"I thought the world of him. I still remember my mother saying to me, 'This is your father.' I remember, too, there was lots of food. And that made me really happy. He was a good man, when he wasn't drinking. But violent when he was." He was also very strict. "He would belt us, or throw things at us. I remember him beating my mother."

It was odd being in the city.

"I noticed everyone was white. The kids across the street would yell 'Yankee, go home' at me. And I saw my first ever blond kids. They'd pull my hair, call me names."

With so many different fathers, Freda's siblings came in very different hues, and Freda was much darker than the brothers and sisters living with her. Fred would try to help. "He'd put me in baths of hot water and Javex and scrub me with a wire brush, especially my knees."

Eventually, her mother tired of the beatings and left Fred. They were very poor then, and she took a waitressing job at a low-end hotel. Freda remembers stealing from the backs of food trucks in order to eat. She also remembers a lot of partying. And phone calls just before closing time, slurred instructions from her mother to clean up last night's garbage before she arrived home with her "guests."

"She'd beat me. See this scar?" She points just over her left eye. "It's from her high heel. She knew if she took me to hospital to get it stitched, they'd probably charge her with child abuse and take me away, so she just packed it with tobacco. And the reason I wear my hair this way is to hide the scars from her hot iron."

One bright spot was that she finally got to meet her older

brothers, who had left the reserve before she was born. "Here were two humongous dark-colored—hurrah, like me!—giants!" They helped out for awhile.

Freda was fourteen, he was nineteen, when she got interested in her first cousin, Bob, and they started dating. He was a rail worker, with a good body and a chronic alcohol problem. A month after they started going out, he abused her for the first time. Like her stepfather, she says, he was a very good man when he wasn't drinking.

"I never had to worry about food, or paying the bills."

By seventeen she was pregnant with the first of three children by him. Bob Junior was seventeen months old when she got pregnant with her second child. She and Bob stayed together eleven years.

Bob was away a lot, working on construction projects, and Freda was lonely. She moved back to the reserve. She boiled the water that collected in a dugout by the road and drank that. She bathed herself and the kids and did laundry in a round metal tub. It was hard going. Bob asked an uncle to help Freda empty the slop pail in the mornings, as they were too heavy for a pregnant woman to be carrying. She had an affair with the uncle that started when she was six months pregnant with the third child.

"Bobby was away so long, I got lonely and vulnerable. Stanley, I called him 'Purple Rose' because he gave me a diamond ring with a purple rose."

She was twenty-two; Stanley was thirty-nine, and married. Life was getting too complicated, so she packed up the car with the kids and what she could carry and headed back to Winnipeg.

Freda wanted to be with Stanley, and she told Bob that she'd been having an affair with him. But somehow, through mixed messages, or maybe it was simply missed opportunity, Stanley thought she had decided not to marry him. He got depressed and shot himself.

Life on the reserve had been one of drinking and drugs. Now in Winnipeg, her life shattered and guilt about the wreckage plaguing her, she really went downhill, becoming —in her own words—a lush, a fleabag. Her family took the kids.

Freda and Bob got back together for a while. He was working on building Portage Place. He was drinking, and beating her so much that it got to the point that he'd hit her for not slicing a sandwich properly. Around the same time, she learned that her three children were deaf, and the youngest was also diagnosed autistic.

Bobby's cousin Curtis rented a room in their Winnipeg apartment. Back then, they'd often all sit around the table drinking. One night, Curtis, saying he was tired of how Bobby treated her, told Freda that Bobby was having an affair. She kicked Bobby out, but not before he had pointed a loaded gun at both her and his cousin.

The downward spiral continued. She knew she couldn't take care of herself, never mind her kids. She signed them over to Children's Aid.

Freda's younger brother was living in a grungy, run-down hotel on Main Street. He'd gotten into the heroin substitutes Talwin and Ritalin. She'd go see him, and he'd be lying in bed with a girl on either side of him, needles and bottles all over the place. She'd been into alcohol more than anything, but was willing to try these new ways of feeling good, of partying. She took up with a junkie that supplied her brother, and at some point they introduced another brother to the needle and cocaine.

She was living in Main Street hotels, and days and nights blurred into each other.

"I regret it now, but at the time I enjoyed the partying."

The times when her head was clear, she knew that losing her children had left a huge void in her life. She figured she needed to fill that space.

"I decided to have Jordan. I knew this guy, a wonderful-looking strawberry blond I'd met when I was still going to school. I asked him to get me pregnant, like a surrogate father, and he did."

But Jordan didn't fill up all the emptiness, and around her, everyone, including her mother, was still partying.

Freda heard about Earl through Bobby's sister.

"He was Polish. After eleven years with a Native, I was gonna try a white guy. I wanted someone to love me. Someone who didn't party all the time. I figured, a guy in jail had to be straight."

She started writing to him, then visiting him at Stony Mountain Penitentiary. And she proposed to him, there in the visitors' room.

"He wasn't a junkie, he had three years' sobriety. From booze and cocaine."

Fourteen months later he was released, and he moved in across the street from her. It wasn't long before they moved in together. He got her smoking cocaine mixed with tobacco—called, unfortunately, "cocoa puffs." Then she graduated to needles.

"All we did was needles. And he started teaching me how to scam. You know, B & Es. Earl would case out a place, I'd wait in the car we stole. He taught me to drive so I'd be able to drive the getaway car. We'd break into a place, he'd go after the booze and crystal, I'd look for the stuff we needed—towels, soap, that kind of stuff."

They'd sell the booze to the owner of a pool hall, who'd buy whatever they had at a premium. Maybe five bucks for a 26-ouncer. It was a turn-on, dangerous and exciting. A real adrenaline rush.

"I didn't think about the people I was robbing. I didn't give a fuck about anyone," she remembers.

"We were staying in this rooming house, him and me. We'd packed a stolen car with stolen electronics and were driving down to Main Street to fence it when the cops started chasing us. It was wild. He turned off real quick and let me out and kept going. A few blocks later they rammed his car and he was busted, but the cops thought the person who'd been with him was a black guy, 'cause I'd been wearing a black leather jacket and a balaclava." Earl got three years, did half that.

Left to herself with only a few dollars and an expensive jacket, she ran into two young girls who taught her all about the ins and outs of prostitution. She'd gotten, if one can, so used to being sexually abused during her mother's parties that selling her body didn't seem so bad. Jordan was staying with her sister, so there was nothing in Freda's life to prevent the steady downward slide. Until the night she was raped. After that, she started going to counselling, trying to understand what had happened to her life, about all the abuse and her reactions to it.

With a straight face, Freda tells me: "After Jordan was born, I figured I'd finished my family planning, and I got my tubes tied. Earl got out of jail, moved in with me, but I threw him out four days later. He was right back into needles." As it turns out, that was all the time she needed to get pregnant, despite the tubal ligation, with her "miracle baby," Earl Junior.

"God meant me to have this child," she says.

Earl's back in jail; this time he got six and a half years. She's hoping he gets his act together during this inarceration, but she tries not to count on it. She has built a home for herself and the two boys, she has remained in contact with the three in Children's Aid, and she has stuck with the counselling.

"Being a nymphomaniac most of my life, I'm trying to stay in control. It's all mind over matter. I was thirty before I had my first orgasm. Earl. He made a woman out of me. I try to think of sex as just another subject in life, like English or French. I need time to heal. I need to feel the way I used to when I was with my grandmother."

She gives me a long, speculative look.

"I'm kinda even thinking of going gay. I never found a guy who wants to settle down."

Oddly, in between the drugs, alcohol, sex and crime, Freda's been a Tupperware lady, and next week there's going to be a party at her place that will be very different from the ones her mother hosted. She'll display the latest in food-saving supplies.

"One thing I learned from white culture—and I learned it while I was working at this upscale restaurant—was the idea of social drinking. You know, a couple of glasses of nice wine with dinner, and leaving it there. Now that I know how to be in society, it's a whole new experience. I feel closer to friends and family."

Freda worked with a group of Native and white people to put on a poverty play, which opened while I was there. It might well have been the first time she'd heard a gathering of people applauding her, liking her. She has a knack for acting: in the play, co-written and directed by Pauline, she becomes a realistic bag lady and narrator. The night of the opening, she coughed a bit, and I told her it added to the realism. She kept it in the next evening.

It took the group about a year of work to develop and produce the play: time to learn about some of the issues that affect the lives of the poor in a broader, less immediate context; time to learn how to work together, how to show up regularly for rehearsals.

No one who participated was told to stop drinking or not to use drugs; the request was simply to postpone such activities until after the meetings and performances. Strategies were put in place to ensure attendance: opening night, two of the directors had the crew and performers to their homes for a pasta dinner and conversation—a nice way of making sure all the players made the curtain.

Whatever else Winnipeg lacks, it does have a sense of community, of disenfranchised people working, living, struggling and discovering together. In their own community, the poor offer no therapy, no grand expectations.

Just acceptance. What all of us crave.

Watching Freda and her two boys walk down the back lane to the waiting cab, it's easy to get fearful and depressed for the three of them. So much damage in her life, and so little good.

A FACT SHEET FROM the Winnipeg Harvest food bank gives these statistics concerning poverty in Manitoba:

- 69,000 children live in poverty—the highest child poverty rate in Canada
- Manitoba has 42,700 people looking for work
- Manitoba has 85,800 people on welfare
- In Manitoba, the average income for a working couple with two children is $57,028
- In Manitoba welfare provides a couple with two children a yearly income of $17,921
- In 1997, the number of persons served by the food bank was 36,800
- 41 percent of food bank users are children

McPhillips Station

THERE'S AN OLD "TWILIGHT ZONE" episode I saw when I was a kid that dealt with slot machines, one-armed bandits. I can't remember the plot, only that it scared the hell out of me.

Pauline and her friends tell me that the McPhillips Station casino is a must-see, an experience I can't miss. Obviously they're not the only ones who feel this way: I've already noticed that the local newspaper has more ads for bingo than it has listings for jobs.

After my limited experience with VLTs in the Edmonton

airport, I'm a bit apprehensive about being "taken over"—the healthy caution one experiences when walking into a cult headquarters. The biggest mistake, or one of the many big mistakes, you can make in life is believing in your own invulnerability. You know: drugs will never run my life; no one can brainwash me; I can stop smoking anytime I want.

I have to carry a large amount of cash with me, because Pauline is away, so it's not safe to leave it at her place. I have the distressing sense that it would be as easy to break into her house as it is to open a cardboard box, and I want to make sure I have enough cash to get home.

This is how I decide to gird myself:
I go hungry—no breakfast, no lunch. My theory is, if I'm hungry, nothing that keeps me from eating will seem that alluring.

I take only half a pack of cigarettes. I'll have to leave to buy smokes, that being the strongest addiction I have, and that should protect me from getting caught up in gambling fever.

I keep fifty bucks distributed in three pockets, the rest buried deep in my knapsack.

If I could carry a crucifix and garlic cloves and a vial of holy water I probably would.

Pauline has told me that at McPhillips Station not long ago infants were found left alone in their parents' cars while they were gambling inside. At least one child has died. Staff now routinely patrol the parking lots, looking to prevent tragedies.

I arrive in a taxi.

At first sight, it looks like one of those Ponderosa steak-houses, with a combination Western and train-station motif. I smoke a cigarette while I, feeling a bit like Freda, case out the place. Although it's a weekday, the parking lot is full. Security is evident. I watch the slow crawl of the house wagon around the perimeter. Looking for abandoned babies, I surmise.

I take a deep breath, throw away my butt and walk inside.

Immediately to my left is the entrance to the slots. Buzzers and bells and the clanging of coins and flashing lights and cigarette smoke. Straight ahead is some crudely robotic "greeter," vaguely reminiscent of the Scarecrow from *The Wizard of Oz*, who bellows what I guess is a recorded welcome at me. I'm walking away when it adds, "I like your hat."

There are some things you shouldn't do to a confirmed crazy person. This is one of them.

I throw off the Rod Serling vibe and realize there's some guy watching from somewhere and talking into a microphone connected to a speaker in this stuffed robot. I refuse to engage in conversation, and quickly walk straight ahead into what appears to be a high-tech bingo parlour.

I don't know how they've managed to keep out the sound of the VLTs, but there's an almost clinical hush in this central area, broken only by the flat voice of the bingo caller. Four or five individuals sit at each round, comfortable booth: each person has his own computer screen and what I guess is an electronic dabber that's applied directly to the screen. It's oddly businesslike. Not much talking, certainly no laughter.

I can't see any empty places. Shrugging, I turn away and walk into the carnival atmosphere of the slot room. I choose a machine—no scientific or superstitious methodology employed here, I just take one of the few empty stools available in one of the long rows.

There are eager, helpful staff everywhere. I trade a twenty-dollar bill for two rows of quarters, telling myself, When these are gone, so am I.

I fumble with the first roll, trying to open it. Not an auspicious beginning. But then I see other players cracking their rolls open on the side of their machines, like you'd crack an egg. Two tries and the quarters spill into my hand and onto the floor. It's really dark below knee level.

I'm feeling a bit conspicuous, bending down and fumbling with change, trying to distinguish quarters from carpet, but finally I'm seated and ready. My machine is the last in a long row. I lose the first roll before I've figured out the machine and gotten into a rhythm. The rhythm, once achieved, is easy: insert coin, coin accepted, spin; insert coin, coin accepted, spin; insert coin, coin accepted, spin. I can't hear the occasional growl of my stomach amid the clang and clatter and buzzers and bells around me.

Unlike some other casinos, this one has no dress code.

And in my row, everyone's smoking steadily, filling up little glass ashtrays that someone comes and replaces with clean ones fairly often.

It seems the customer can have no working-class habit that's not tolerated, and cleaned up after, with relentless goodwill. It's a little like the voluntary-euthanasia clinics in *Brave New World.*

My back is starting to bother me, which I feel is all to the good—yet another protection against too prolonged a stay. I try to look professionally competent as I crack the second roll smartly on the metal edge of the catch-all tray below my machine; the third crack spills out the quarters and I leave the majority of coins there, scooping up small handfuls as need dictates.

I decide to get serious, and try to understand when and how and how much this VLT pays off. It occurs to me that the jackpots advertised—50,000, 20,000 and so on—are not in dollars but in quarters.

Insert coin, coin accepted, spin, insert coin . . .

There's a lady beside me, just took over an abandoned stool, who presses spin and pulls the protruding handle energetically down. I thought the arm was just for show, but it apparently works. I stick with the buttons.

I start getting payoffs—small, embarrassingly small at first, a few paltry coins clattering down. Adding to my pile.

Insert coin, coin accepted, spin; insert coin, coin accepted, spin; insert coin . . .

A healthier-sounding payoff, looks like I've doubled my stake. I start worrying about how I'll carry all these quarters out. Some people have little buckets and I want one too, but I have to insert coin, coin accepted, spin, insert coin. Halfway through my second roll, I too start turning my head in the direction of major payoffs, anything lasting more than a few seconds. I am not an envious person as a rule, but I have to admit to feeling just a little pang as I step up my own pace, insert coin. It occurs to me that these are the only machines I've ever dealt with in my life that work consistently. If you've ever tried to get a cup of coffee, a newspaper, subway tokens, or a can of pop out of a vending machine, you know what I'm talking about.

Insert coin, coin accepted, spin; insert coin . . . I have no idea what time it is, how long I've sat here. Have you noticed how we rarely display clocks in public any more?

I hear a guy telling his wife, "You've got to work these machines into a payoff mode." I wait, interested, for further details, but none are forthcoming. That's okay, I'll just step up the pace.

Quite suddenly, I've used up the two rolls. Damn. I sit there for a moment, flummoxed. Sure, I tell myself, I could leave if I wanted to, but I have a feeling that if I run the machine a little longer, that elusive payoff mode will kick in. Shame to leave now. The insert coin sign is lit. I can't leave the stool, someone else will grab the machine I've spent twenty dollars priming.

I'm feeling oddly panicky, looking around me, needing more quarters. I see a staff person and wave frantically. She sees me, she's coming. She's taking too long. My rhythm is broken. A swift exchange of twenty for two more rolls. No mucking about now. Crack one open, insert coin, coin accepted . . .

I'm grateful.

This roll lasts a little longer, augmented by a fifty-quarter payoff, then another, smaller one. I have a hoard, a small mountain of quarters; I can play forever.

I don't do the math. Translate the quarters into dollars. That would sound much less impressive.

Forty quarters clatter their way down to me. I really like that sound, when it's drawn out and substantial. Lacking a bucket, I stash quarters in various pockets, leaving enough in the tray to be able to insert coin, coin accepted, spin, insert coin . . .

Even though it's a noisy, crowded, smoky place (I'm down to six cigarettes now), the space between my body and the machine is quiet, hushed, expectant.

I suppose it's natural to humanize these things. People call their cars by pet names, I cross my fingers when I turn on my computer at home. The machine and I are pals, of a sort. It wants to please me. I feed it, don't I? And I don't let any time at all elapse before insert coin and coin accepted.

My back hurts. My stomach is uncomfortably empty.

I'm aware that the woman at the next stool is gone. People come and go here so quickly—you'd think they'd know better than to abandon a well-prepped machine. I pop a quarter in that one, feeling oddly like a sneak thief, but nothing happens except insert coin.

I'm hoping my machine didn't notice the small interruption.

A couple, mother and son maybe, stop. She says, "This is a good machine," and sits. She's teaching the boy—he's certainly over eighteen—how to play. I think briefly of Freda and her brothers: Here's a good drug, this is how to inject it.

She tells him not to take it too seriously, just have some fun.

I'm using quarters from my pockets now. That twenty went by so swiftly, even with the wins. Insert coin, coin accepted, spin; insert coin, coin accepted, spin; insert coin . . .

It doesn't feel like money, more like pellets to feed the machine. An annoyance getting between me and the spin mechanism.

Out of the corner of my eye, along the row perpendicular to me, I catch sight of Kirk, a young aboriginal man. He acted in the poverty play, as the ruler of a kingdom suspiciously like Winnipeg, strutting around the stage dressed in a glittery robe and crown. He's at a stool in front of one of the poker machines, facing into the crowd. In his hand are crumpled bills. He exchanges them for a single roll and turns to face the machine. Not interrupting my own play, I watch him, wondering why he thinks he can beat the odds. I suspect he's using the money he made last night for the play. I know it wasn't a lot. The first night was the best attended, and even then the actors collected only eighteen dollars apiece.

I can't let my attention wander. Insert coin. A few minutes later, and Kirk is standing beside me, looking shocked to see me here.

"Ah, it's research, Kirk," I explain, not quite believing it any more myself. He bums a cigarette, which really pulls me up short. In the hierarchy of addictions, smoking is king. That he would feed a poker machine before his nicotine habit indicates a serious problem. People buy cigarettes before buying groceries. I use his presence as an excuse to by two more rolls, one for him and one for me.

He loses his quickly, and comes to say goodbye. Though I resent the interruption, I try not to show it. Having just enjoyed the sound of quarters raining down into the tray, I'm feeling like I'm finally on a roll. It doesn't occur to me that I've blown the equivalent of two cartons of cigarettes, while occasionally winning enough to buy a couple of disposable lighters.

It's odd when the all the quarters finally disappear. It must be a mistake, I think, rechecking my pockets. The relationship between me and the machine, the intimacy and promise of Jackpot! and Win! Win! Win! was illusory. Fake. What's even odder is that, for a moment, I feel blameworthy for not being able to respond to that insert coin light. I know I have to leave. I know equally well that the moment I do, some stranger will come, insert coin and win what is due to me. I'm frozen with indecision. Just go. Don't look back, don't see what happens. Just leave the area.

It's like I'm velcroed to the stool. I rip myself away and like Lot—never looking back—make it out of the room and into the comparative quiet of the bingo parlour. This time I notice, at one end, a small McDonald's, which effectively reminds me how hungry I am. This is working-class heaven—or hell. I eat a Quarter-Pounder with Cheese and a milkshake, and wonder about cigarettes, now that I'm out. It seems to me that a place like this wouldn't want people leaving to buy the necessities of life, so I wander around till I come to a gift shop. Sure enough, I'm able to buy smokes, but what breaks the spell utterly for me is the layout of lottery tickets under clear plastic on the counter. Just in case you still have any cash.

I CALLED PAULINE AT the end of the summer for an update on her campaign. Although the run-up to the election officially started on September 15, she had already been knocking on doors in her community and visiting senior citizens' homes.

When I asked her what she found surprising, she didn't have to think long for an answer. In the last election, only

30 percent of the eligible electorate in her ward voted. Poor people are so divorced from our collective version of democracy that they simply cannot see any connection to the daily, often grim, realities of their lives. And no one has tackled this political illiteracy, seen it as important enough, urgent enough, to rank alongside learning to read and write.

"All these good people in our helping systems are totally preoccupied with providing daily sustenance to their clients, but never in a political context, never as something the client can and should affect."

Powerless people react in powerless ways.

Known in her community, admired by diverse groups, she was able to get 167 individuals, mostly the poor, working on her campaign, believing that it just might be possible.

"You should have seen it," she later tells me, after the election is over. "Single mothers pushing strollers, knocking on doors, trying to get the vote out. People who usually prefer not to be noticed, out to make a difference."

The man who encouraged her to run is being touted as the first out gay mayor in Canada, and she's thrilled about his victory.

For her own race, even though the vote was held on Welfare Cheque day, they pulled out a lot of the vote of the disenfranchised—a miracle, in the truest sense.

The final tally: votes cast for the incumbent, 4,433; votes cast for Pauline, 4,033.

A loss, but also a big win. They came very close. They politicized a community used to passivity. And there is always next time.

CHAPTER FOUR

TORONTO

At home in the Annex

HOW DOES THE LARGEST city in Canada treat its poor? When there are more resources, are fewer people left to fend for themselves?

In a way.

I'm walking down Lowther Avenue to Avenue Road, past expensive houses and dead gardens and those odd-looking purple heads of cabbage the rich seem to favour—perhaps it's a subconscious association with Lewis Carroll and the old rhyme that pairs *cabbages* with *kings*.

Just before the intersection, I have to wait while a crane swings a large load of debris from the stackable "condominium mansions" under construction over to a battered pick-up truck. This is an island of unapologetic conspicuous consumption, and I turn a graceless 360-degree pirouette to see what vistas the mansion-dwellers will enjoy from their windows. Yorkville shops, Bloor Street shops, the Four Seasons Hotel, gracious dining, two specialty stores offering the best cigars only steps away—it is indeed a wonderful life.

On Cumberland Street, people meander. None of that choking, teeming, elbow-jarring Eaton Centre shopping nonsense. No fuming by a cash register waiting for an employee to deign to notice you.

I cross over to a stylized park, and sit down on one of the benches scattered around.

The powers-that-be haven't yet demolished the brick façade of the University Theatre that fronts onto Bloor Street, behind me; it still looks like an abandoned studio set. I've grown fond of it. Across the street, women are framed in the window of an upscale hairstylist, pampered and indulged and fussed over.

On the bench closest to Bloor, a woman, perhaps in her sixties, sits. At first glance she seems to be enjoying the mild weather and reading her paper. Shoppers leaving Yorkville walk by her, caught up in their busy lives.

She is wearing a long grey coat, the kind that promises to

keep you warm, and grey jogging pants. On her head is a black stocking hat, and on her feet are running shoes. It's how she turns the pages of the paper that initially catches my attention. There's something Victorian, even patrician about her: portrait of a lady reading.

Focusing more intently, though, I can see that the paper is a tabloid, a few weeks old at least, stained and torn. Her hands have that tell-tale grey-black varnish that speaks of long weeks without access to a shower, without a place to reclaim oneself. But her face. Her face is steeled, steeled against despair, against a desperation held private and felt to be shameful.

A neighbour of mine was recently returning from a Yorkville hairdresser and, walking along Bloor Street, stopped in front of a woman huddled over a small cardboard sign.

"I couldn't see her face. In front of her was a tin with nickels and pennies and I wondered, who gives like that?"

"It's likely her own change, she was priming the pump."

"Oh. Anyway, I'm standing in front of her, here I am just coming from Yorkville, and not only do I have a house, I have two. I look for change and all I have is a two-dollar coin so I lean forward and put it in the tin, and she looks up at me and smiles and says, sweetly, 'Thanks for stopping by.' Just from the way she said it, you could tell that she had a good upbringing. I felt so helpless. What are we supposed to do?"

The mayor of Toronto would find her perfectly acceptable. Discreet in her poverty, homelessness and need. Fending for herself, getting what she needs where she can find it, an embodiment of the trickle-down economy.

It always comes as a shock, these glimpses of how far we've deteriorated as a society. And how pathetic, how late and inadequate, are our civic responses. City politicians are reassessing when to call a cold-weather alert—that moment when the blood freezes and people die. Minus 15 Celsius used to be the temperature that moved us to compassion, but now Environment Canada will look at wind chill and other factors.

Two articles recently placed side by side on the Greater Toronto page of the *Toronto Star* illustrate our inability to prioritize our responses to urgent need:

A homeless man died of hypothermia early yesterday, and this is "a harbinger of things to come," a Toronto councillor says.

Councillor Jack Layton said the 1,200 hostel spaces for homeless males are already filled, and the local churches' Out of the Cold program doesn't start for a few weeks.

"We're in a very grim situation here and it could be our worst winter for homeless people," said Layton.

The temperature had dropped to 7 Celsius. Layton issued an "urgent call" to the real estate industry to help.

"We need immediately space for about 600 beds
in order to deal with the backlog," he said.
—*Toronto Star, October 3, 1998*

And:

> Toronto city council has given its "final blessing"
> to the design of a suicide-prevention barrier along
> the Bloor Viaduct . . .
> At its July 8 meeting, council approved $1.5 mil-
> lion to build the barrier.
>
> *—Bruce DeMara,*
> *Toronto Star, October 3, 1998*

THERE'S A BIG PARK DOWNTOWN, the home of Allan Gardens, that was once a tourist attraction. It's less popular these days, now that it is occupied by the destitute and homeless. I lived for a time across the street from it. There's a danger here, an unpredictability more common to the jungle than to a city. A sense that the man smiling at you could just as easily cut your throat, with no change in the expression on his face.

Nights are filled with hellish sounds: shrieks of pain and rage, dark humourless laughter. Hookers, crack dealers and their customers own the park. Regular people have learned, the hard way, to stay away.

There once seemed to be an informal agreement to leave the park to the "real people" during the day, but that no longer applies. I sit on a bench one afternoon and watch the action. Human wreckage sprawls on the grass, some with bottle-shaped brown paper bags they argue and wrestle over, some asleep. Along the footpaths, other people are returning home from work, tired and unhappy-looking. Some glare at the messy, distasteful display of humanity; others avert their eyes and pick up their pace.

Shelters don't open till later in the evening. Drop-in centres don't permit the drunk or the stoned inside. People don't know this, they only know that their park is infested with unsavory elements, their neighbourhood is ruined.

Every few minutes, another man stands up, casually picks a tree and urinates against it. Imagine having to live your whole life, every aspect of it, in full public view.

There's a fellow I know who panhandles along Bloor Street near Bedford Road, edging up to the upscale Yorkville shopping area. He stakes his territory near a hot dog stand, a couple of phone booths, in an area bordered by a stone wall. He looks like a wild man, his hair matted and tangled, his pants dragged down under the soles of his feet, most days covered only with socks. But he is surprisingly pleasant and soft-spoken, and he tries hard to keep track of a conversation and keep up his end. Some days he's too delusional to follow, lost in his own world. There is a dignity about him, though, as pathetic and lost as he is, that transcends his appearance and circumstances.

Walking down Bloor Street one afternoon, I see him curled up on the sidewalk, right up against the wall. His eyes are closed, one hand is down his pants, clearly wrapped around his penis. People are cutting wide swaths around him. It's one thing to be homeless, quite another to be masturbating in public. There are things we don't like our children to see.

I pause, unsure what to do, not wanting to leave him in danger of being busted for public indecency, not wanting to embarrass him. I end up crouching beside his head, and I tap him gently on the shoulder. His eyes fly open in alarm, startled out of his reverie, and the hand that had been clenching and unclenching spasmodically in his pants is swiftly pulled out.

"Hi." I smile at him, seeing nothing I shouldn't.

He struggles to sit up. "Hello. How're you? Are you okay?"

"I'm great. It's getting cold, though. I wondered if you'd like a coffee."

I slip him some change, and we smoke together for a few minutes until I'm sure he's back in the world, and defensively aware of his surroundings.

Our very first conversation was about cigarettes, in fact. I'd gone up to him and asked if he had enough cigarettes, intending to give him half my pack. Instead, he reached into his pocket and pulled out a crumpled pack of Camel filters, which he offered to me. You've got to love a guy like that.

I remember ducking into the alcove of a fast food establishment, joining him for a moment, out of the rain. While we were chatting, a woman opened the inside door, an effort made awkward by the fact that her hands were holding a pop and a hamburger, which she thrust towards him with an unpleasant mix of anger and charity. He smiled at her, a kind smile, and said, "No, thank you."

At that moment, he personified all the dignity in the world.

THERE WAS A SKIT I watched once on the Comedy Channel, from an old "In Living Color" episode, in which a woman pretending to be Carole King is trying to write a song for the album Tapestry. In order to get to work, she has to cut off the young man who is seeking her help, giving him the bum's rush out the front door, which she locks after him. Then she busies herself strumming the first few lines of "You've Got a Friend."

Outside, the young man is held up, mugged, beaten bloody while crying out, "Carole, help!" repeatedly. She closes the window to cut off the noise, and gets the refrain:

"You just call out my name . . . "

"Carole!"

"And you know wherever I am . . . "

Stabbed by his assailant, one last pleading cry over the refrain goes unnoticed.

Our helping systems are a lot like that, busily engaged in self-congratulatory back-slapping, fundraising and feeling good about their efforts. Meanwhile, back in the ghetto . . .

Compared to the general population, homeless people face a much higher risk of premature death, higher rates of infectious disease, acute illness and chronic conditions, and more dental problems. They are prone to higher rates of injury and violence, and a higher risk of suicide, mental health problems, or alcohol or substance abuse. Homelessness also contributes to the development of treatment-resistant tuberculosis and other diseases such as Hepatitis C and HIV/AIDS.
— *Breaking the Cycle of Homelessness,*
Interim Report of the Mayor's Homelessness Action
Task Force, Toronto, July 1998

THERE'S AN INTERESTING AND theatrical gauntlet for shoppers this afternoon on Bloor Street near Spadina. Backs against a wall, six men sit on the cold pavement; at least three of them are already quite drunk. Opposite them, two men are perched on the edge of a concrete planter, while a third looms over them. From across the street, I notice a middle-aged white guy speaking forcefully to them. He's fairly well dressed. I can't tell what he's saying to them, but their facial expressions range from bemusement to aggravation.

I cross at the lights, curious, but he's already leaving as I reach the group, and looking a bit smug and self-satisfied to boot.

"What was he telling you?" I ask the guys at the planter.

This produces an explosion of commentary.

"What wasn't he telling us?"

"He's been just like us."

"Lost his job."

"Lost his kids to Children's Aid because of his drinking."

"And then his dog died."

"Lost his damn cat probably too. Jesus."

"Wants us to go to AA."

"We said, buy us a bottle, we'll hold our own damn AA meeting."

"Yeah, he wouldn't though."

Productive citizens, the "real" people, are alternately cajoled and harangued as they duck through the gauntlet. Some show clearly their anger and resentment. Some sprinkle change. A woman thrusts two shiny red apples at the guy I'm talking too, Cody; he munches on one of them while stuffing the other in his pocket, telling me this is his job, and how many people could bring themselves to do it?

"You gotta be humble, holding out your hand to people. Some are rude, some mean, some don't even answer you. They can knock your spirits down, but they haven't got our dignity. I know, for me, I won't go any lower than this. They won't make me crawl. I wouldn't fuck queers for money, I'd shoot myself first. I had a buddy who went that low, ended up hanging himself in prison. Takes more courage to live than to die."

He gets the odd paying job. He can earn forty or fifty bucks beating up on people. He'll be in a bar, and someone will say, "Cody, get that guy," and he's big and strong enough to do it. His knuckles are bruised and cut.

"When I get paid, I'll always bring a bottle by for these guys. They're pissed off that the Fort York shelter has closed down.

"At Fort York, staff didn't fuck with us. We could come and go, have a drink, you know, do what we do best. Go in, get warm. We're up all night, and still tired and bored in the morning." He laughs.

One stocky, belligerent fellow with a freshly scarred face leaves his place on the sidewalk to confront me. Already intoxicated, he demands to know where he's seen me before. Cody stiffens, ready to pummel his friend, perhaps for the second time, but I joke with the guy, and he smiles, disarmed.

Beside Cody is a man who has only recently returned to the street. Kicked out by his girlfriend. He has long, clean hair, his clothes are still presentable, but he has no welfare-acceptable identification. He's here from Winnipeg.

"Sure I want a job. But I have no bus tickets, not even money to get something to eat, no house, no phone. Who's going to hire me?"

Cody's heard a bit about Y2K, or I suspect that's what he means when he starts talking about how Armageddon is coming soon.

"We'll be happy then. There won't be such a big gap between people. All of a sudden everyone will be poor together, united again."

Hey, you've got to have hope.

"I WANTED TO MEET Jesus, so for about a year I swallowed fifty boxes of salt, you know, the regular boxes."

"What? You dissolved it in water? Drank it?"

"No." He laughs, holding his hand high above his mouth in a pouring gesture. "Just like this. Then, after my heart attack, I still wanted to meet Jesus. I wanted to ask him to cure my schizophrenia. But, when I saw him, He said, 'I love you just the way you are.' He touched me here, right here on the shoulder. He said, 'Nine more years.' You know the Lotto 6/49? That's what He meant. I'll win it in nine years. Then I'm outta here."

He's a big bear of a guy, holding forth to a small audience of smokers in front of a squat grey structure on the grounds of the Queen Street Mental Health Centre, a large psychiatric hospital in Toronto recently merged with the Clarke Institute, the Addiction Research Foundation and the Donwoods Institute to form the new mega-corp, the Centre for Addictions and Mental Health.

The building is one of the rotating venues of the four-year-old Out of the Cold program, organized by churches and neighbourhood groups to feed and provide temporary shelter for the homeless in the winter months, giving those who are unwelcome anywhere else a chance to get inside. I'm here feeling prickly, ready to take (and give) offence should I get a whiff of the "Aren't we wonderful to be so charitable?" vibe.

My friend Nora McCabe is someone who spends the winter trying to save the lives of those we've collectively failed. It's October, and her team is gearing up for its Sunday night rotation. So far, I've run into only the patrons themselves, who, despite the fact that it's only 5:30 and supper's not served till 6:00, are already arriving in ones and twos—some staggering, some limping badly, all underdressed for the occasion.

The smokers are waiting outside, time for one last cigarette. One senior fellow draped in a raincoat older than he is picks up the conversation. Incongruously, he has a small bottle with an Evian label peeking out of his pocket, but if that's water I'll eat my hat. I am uncomfortably aware that if I were here as a staff member, I'd be telling him to open the bottle so I could smell it, confiscate it.

There are so many here who would be escorted out of any established agency in the city—for being drunk, or openly drinking, for a history of aggressive behaviour, or for drug use. That's why they're here, of course, because our gatekeepers have barred the doors, not overly concerned about where else these folks can go. The agencies have their rules. And rules assume paramount importance, even over the lives and deaths of those who break them. I've been in places where the posted rules outnumber the participants. The rules here are simple: no drinking, no weapons, no swearing (I assume that means loudly and abusively), no smoking inside.

The fellow in the raincoat and a friend were just at the hospital dropping off "an old drunk who kept passing out." He declares the Scott Mission the best mission in the city, but he hasn't been able to go for seven or eight months. "There's a guy there, big guy, likes to use me for a punching bag. Don't know why. People don't let you alone. Twice today I almost got beat up."

A man with a scarf tied around his forehead comes crashing out of the doorway in a blur and grabs him by the front of his raincoat, leans his face real close to the old man's. "And here's number three, you old bastard!" He roars out a laugh, embraces him, then wanders off, still laughing.

Nobody here throws away a smoke until the filter itself is burning, or, if it's a rollie, until their lips start to burn. Waste not.

When we actually get inside, it's the volunteers who look most out of place. Not that we're talking about a collection of Lady Bountifuls, although part of me tries to be prepared for that. These are just plain folk with everyday burdens, some economically better off than others, but nobody shining with missionary zeal or avid Christianity.

Yesterday, I warily watched the volunteer training session

in the big room where guests will be laying out exercise mats on the floor after dinner is finished, and heard the old hands describe the "routine" and pitch for their particular shifts. (Each one, we're told, has its own attractions and drawbacks.)

Ann Beach, who was once my own physician, took the floor for the *de rigueur* public health lecture. In my defensiveness—born of pure overidentification with the target group—I was sure the emphasis would be on how not to catch anything from the homeless. In fact, she seemed more worried about the homeless catching something from the volunteers: she stressed the importance of the volunteers washing their hands frequently, of the need to cover their mouths when coughing or sneezing, and how to keep the food-preparation counters sterilized.

It was all so chillingly practical. I found myself feeling somewhat histrionic as I wondered whether we've all gone mad, whether anyone else out in the world is thinking of all the horrors we've come to accept as everyday.

In a small lounge beside the main area, there are rows of chairs facing the television. One minute I look in and there are just two people; the next it's standing room only. Only the overnight guests are allowed to sit in there. Those who've come for supper are leaning against the wall in the corridor, some sitting, most standing.

I look at the faces, some with downcast eyes—shame or

anger—some with a weariness beyond fixing, some in another world, where pain can be kept at bay by whatever intoxicant is at hand.

Laughter, barely controlled hysteria, gushes out of one man, who reddens and leaves to pace around, looking for control. But there is, on the whole, remarkably good cheer among the men and women here. More than I would be able to muster in the same circumstances.

A well-meaning, emotionally fragile woman tells me with some pride that she has announced in the mall of the Queen Street Mental Hospital, a gathering place for various in-patients, that supper is available at six. I bite back my smile, envisioning my friend Nora's eye-roll when she hears that the program is taking a load off the hospital's food budget. "Good for you," I say.

A street-wise, angry woman can be heard talking about all the "headcases and nutbars" hanging around, in a way that suggests "there goes the neighbourhood." One group will always persecute another, at every level of society, working out hierarchies of intolerance.

Back in the lounge, a young man with large stitches across the flat of his nose coughs violently. A middle-aged couple sit at the back. I saw them here last year. She's a diabetic. Her condition used to be controlled through diet and pills, but it's hard to eat right, hard to buy the kind of food she needs, so now she's on insulin. The government pays for the blood-tester and the hypodermics. Food she's got to take care of herself.

Another couple walked here from St. George and Bloor. She has just had a cast taken off her leg (drank too much and fell down, she giggles) and still leans on a crutch. Seven months ago, she arrived by bus from Oshawa. Met her friend—he had a broken leg then too!—who was staying in Seaton House, a men's hostel. They've been together ever since.

The program has found its own regulars, people who return year after year after year, people whose situations have not improved in all the in-between months. Nora finds it terrible and sad that on opening night these same regulars will ask her politely how her summer went. As though they were meeting on equal ground, at a party or other get-together, not at a stopgap overnight shelter which is all our society is equipped to offer them.

The dining room/bedroom is empty, except for the bustle of volunteers. The green board against the wall carries a message and the menu:

WELCOME.
TONIGHT'S MENU:
SCOTCH BROTH, ROAST BEEF, POTATOES,
VEGETABLES, SALAD, HOME BAKING

Tables are pushed together in long rows. Each table has overflowing bread baskets and bowls of celery sticks, carrots

and bread-and-butter pickles, along with settings of real cut-
lery, glasses and napkins.

In the kitchen, gravy is being stirred slowly. A call goes out
to the potato-mashers, while others pull out and start slicing
the roast beef.

One of the volunteers, a lovely, frail-looking older woman
I'll call Marian, who is an in-patient at the hospital, glides
around wanting to help but feeling a little out of place, I suspect. When I say to her, "That roast beef looks really good,
eh?" she responds with some alarm.

"That's not roast beef. They say it is, but I knew that lady
they're cooking. She was a fine woman."

I do some loose translation in my head and figure I'm
being told she's not feeling a part of this and doesn't quite
know what to do with her feelings of discomfort.

"Well, why don't you try the desserts?" I suggest lamely.
"They look pretty good."

She smiles at me and wanders over to that table.

By 6:05, every chair is taken. Soup is up first, brought to
the tables on serving trays by the volunteers.

I sit for a while with Rudy—we both lived in the same
Parkdale boarding home till he got himself evicted—and his
friend, a nattily dressed man who keeps his scarf, hat and over-
coat on throughout the meal. He's having a bitch of a time trying to get the spoon to his mouth with at least some soup still
in it.

"He's Yugoslavian, just like me," says Rudy.

For something to do, I tear up a piece of bread and chew while I ask what's causing the shakes.

"Medication," the old fellow says.

Rudy says indignantly, "They tried to make me like that! Fuck 'em!"

Rudy has a room now at Keele Street and St. Clair Avenue, which swallows most of his cheque. Eating means bouncing around from place to place.

I move over to where the big Jesus-seeker sits, shovelling in dinner. I tell him this is one table that doesn't have to look for the salt. He brays out crumbs and laughter.

"That's right. Just turn me upside down and shake me!"

There's a man at the table who's been homeless since his ex-girlfriend used the welfare "snitch line" to get even; this service allows you to turn in someone you're angry with for "fraud" or "abuse of welfare." Welfare now says he owes them $180. Another man was cut off when he couldn't fulfill the requirement to hand in job-search forms—he's illiterate but likes to keep that to himself.

I see Marian over by herself against the wall, looking a little desperate and, I fear, hungry. I wander over and say to her, "Hey, you know, there's no one in the bread. I tried it."

"You didn't eat it with butter?" she asks in a horrified voice.

I hasten to reassure her. "Nope, just plain."

A kind of beatific relief spreads over her face, making me

glad, and I resume my table-hopping. There's a guy I first met at an aboriginal women's shelter, where he taught crafts. He's been homeless for a while, but tries to reassure me, and himself, that he should be able to pull himself together by next month.

Another fellow, whose healthy complexion causes him to be mistaken for a volunteer, shrugs his shoulders in a "shit happens" gesture. "Last year this time I was in Greece." He says he lost his job as a financial analyst and gravitated to Parkdale. With him is a sprightly lady who, before, worked as a secretary. She had hoped not to need these meals this year but considers herself lucky to have a place to come.

I wander again, and against the far wall come upon an instructive scene. A large man, in his late twenties or early thirties, is standing hunched in fury with clenched fists, his chair knocked over on the floor behind him, his ski jacket dripping with coffee. Someone whispers to me that another man flung his coffee at the guy, then took off.

The victim looks around, absolutely ready to lose it, to pour out invective, to throw a tantrum, to toss furniture around. In any other agency dealing with the poor, the crazy, the addicted, the homeless, a battle royal would have erupted. Staff would have become involved, appealed to as if they were playground supervisors, expected to punish, to bar.

I remember how, when I worked at the drop-in in Parkdale, a place for discharged psychiatric survivors to hang out in the daytime, grown men, tough-looking and street-wise, would come find me with small complaints, roughly the equivalent of "He touched me, make him stop touching me" or "He called me a name, make him stop." It embarrasses me to think of it now, but I believed that they were choosing to act like kindergarten kids; I didn't realize that it was in fact the workers who were acting like kindergarten cops, thus creating and sustaining their clients' powerlessness, the constant "come fix this" appeal that workers so often thrive on.

As I watch this man, he takes control of himself, a herculean effort worthy of a standing ovation, and ends the episode by taking himself into the washroom and cleaning off his jacket. He appreciates where he is. He appreciates that volunteers are treating him and others with respect, and that that respect obligates him in turn to behave in a way that demonstrates that he is worthy of it.

The volunteers continue serving, respectful and just a little frantic, as pleased with the selection of desserts as the recipients. Those who have a place to go for the night are starting the long walk home. Others are lining up for their mats, staking out a few feet of turf to lay them on. Most will be asleep by 9:00 p.m. It's exhausting, being homeless, just surviving on the streets.

In the kitchen, Hank and Pat are already working on preparing breakfast—eggs, homefries, toast—while others are making sandwiches for the lunches that will be handed out as the guests leave.

Marian is sitting by herself at a now empty table. Before her is a full plate, just brought to her by a smiling volunteer. I watch as she stares at it a moment, then, perhaps deciding that charitable acts differ somehow from simple charity, starts to eat, smiling.

It is particularly poignant to me that the volunteer staff here don't want to usurp the role of paid workers. They don't seem to realize that most of their "guests" have worn out their welcome at agencies, or have broken the rules or failed to fill out the forms—it is usually a combination of this and worker preference for the easier-to-handle that ensures their abandonment.

The volunteers have given considerable thought to the consequences of what they are doing to keep people from dying. Ontario Premier Mike Harris has claimed that volunteerism can fill any vacuum created by the cutbacks to welfare and social agencies, pointing to people and programs such as this as evidence of success. These volunteers don't want to give him more justification for his disastrous cuts. And they know, better than most, how little impact they are making towards getting and keeping people off the street. There was a time when we provided hostel beds; now we hand out sleeping bags for people to lay over the snow.

THE POOR DON'T GET TO choose the kinds of workers, or the type of help, they need. There is no say in how that help is delivered to them, during what hours, or with what attitude. Powerlessness, which so much defines their everyday existence, is exacerbated and prolonged in each social service contact. As are shame and humiliation.

Our failures are by now more numerous than our successes. And the gulf between clients and staff, between academic knowledge and the reality of the street, yawns wide.

The system is now set up more for the purposes of judging the worthiness of the poor than for providing services to all those who clearly need them. The more people on the streets, the more men and women in need, the greater the opportunity for the agencies to pick and choose who will benefit from their limited services. And human nature being what it is, the chosen will be the "deserving"—those who the worker can identify with, those who don't make waves, those who are polite and thankful, those who aren't inebriated or on drugs. This creates a dangerous caste system in our provision of help.

For example, the target population for an agency might be the traditional street-dwellers, alcoholic men in their fifties and sixties who've spent so long in this "lifestyle" that they don't really remember any other. We'll establish hostels, the hostels will hire staff, the staff will create rules barring clients who show up drunk. And when one or two freeze to death, we'll talk about gaps, and falling through the net, and maybe set up more hostel beds and more exclusionary rules. Finally, those who are most in need are conveniently and fatally ignored.

I have had the opportunity to visit many different agencies, psychiatric hospitals and shelters across the country, and to speak to staff and clients at these diverse places. I've been fortunate enough to have sat for a time with activists from other areas—AIDS, physical disabilities, the fragile elderly—and to have seen for myself the efforts of activists working with the "simply poor." I have learned that the distinction we create among the various groups in need are artificial and serve mainly to keep people in the boxes we've prepared for them. As well, they enable the funding bodies to foster competition for the few dollars thrown their way, ensuring a kind of agency jingoism, a separateness and lack of co-ordination that militates against client relief.

Any activist who challenges the status quo, who confronts an agency or its staff where policy is concerned, bears the brunt of its indignation, achieving only yet another label, yet another rejection. Challenge is never viewed positively, rarely if ever seen as an opportunity to learn and grow; challenge is a threat to agency well-being and staff self-image, both of which have grown comfortably secure over years of "service." Therefore the challenger must be dealt with, silenced or isolated or simply barred, if manipulation or co-option proves ineffective.

I sometimes wonder how many potential leaders in our leadership-starved communities have been thoroughly discouraged and demoralized before reaching their full capability, sacrificed to the orderly and routine workings of the system.

I'M WALKING DOWN THE corridor of the Addiction Research
Foundation in Toronto, talking with Bill Currie, its former
chair, who is currently heading up the board of the newly
merged Centre for Addictions and Mental Health. I tell him
about my Vancouver experience—the open-air drug markets,
people buying and selling drugs within sight of a police station—and then I relate what happened to me just recently
when I took a cigarette break during a committee meeting
outside this same building.

"So I watch a cab pull up, a guy leaps out, bounds up the
stairs, pulling bills out of his wallet, and asks me, 'Where's
the methadone clinic?' I gotta ask, Bill, what the hell's the
difference?"

One of the reasons I like Bill is that he can recognize
absurdity when he hears it, and his head-shaking laughter
shows that he is not a captive to institutional correctness.
Considering that his day job involves being the Ontario
Provincial Police's Regional Commander for the Greater
Toronto Area (GTA), a population of 6.5 million people, that's
saying something. He also serves on the Mayor's Homelessness
Action Task Force, established by Mel Lastman and chaired by
Anne Golden.

We've established an unusual degree of rapport since our
first board meeting, during which I asked, in keeping with my
tendency to be occasionally obstreperous, whether or not he
came to the table armed. I've yet to see him in uniform, but

he has all the right bells and whistles, including a whipcord antenna, in his car.

"I'm an atypical cop," he admits, explaining that he was a teacher, then a vice-principal at inner-city schools, before deciding, at the age of thirty-four, to become a police officer.

"I didn't join at eighteen—that isn't all I know. I'm really aware of the role of the police in relation to the community and how we should interact.

"The public wants to know, 'How do we take a person on the street, and move them right through the system to self-sufficiency?' The question is that simple, and that complex."

Bill says the causes of homelessness are more complicated than they appear—an idea I've always resisted.

"As you backtrack through people's lives, looking at how they came to this—it could be a lost job, illness, addiction—it's like entering the wide mouth of a funnel, and nothing happens, there's no intervention, so you drop out the bottom. We have to help those people, and we have to prevent others from entering the funnel in the first place. The homeless I've spoken to—whether in agencies, drop-ins or under the Gardiner Expressway—basically what they say they want is dignity and security."

He doesn't believe homelessness is a chosen lifestyle, as some politicians like to suggest. His first impression of how people make it off the street? "It seems to me that we've established a system that's based on luck. The client is either lucky or unlucky, and some people are really unlucky."

He describes listening to a fellow tell how he and his friend were just lying around a park, when this fellow heard about a program, and his life just took off. "I wanted to ask, 'What about that friend who was with you? What's he doing, where is he now?' This whole helping industry is disconnected, uncoordinated, like a string of lights on a Christmas tree— everybody puts a bulb in, but if even one doesn't work, none of them do."

Three levels of government are failing to coordinate their approaches and funding.

"We're investing significant dollars into the system. We must have coordination, we must avoid duplication." But the system, by its nature, encourages agencies to branch out beyond their mandates by fostering competition for scarce funding. "The existing agency will identify a gap, and apply for and receive funding to fill that gap, never mind whether someone else could have done it better. You can't really blame the agencies, they're just trying to stay alive, but you can't build an effective system based on the grant structure of the moment."

According to the report of the Homelessness Action Task Force, there are sixty-five community mental health agencies in the GTA, and thirty-four community addiction agencies.

"People who work in the addiction and mental health fields agree that Toronto does not have a co-ordinated service delivery system. Homeless people generally have no one to help them navigate the system or to advocate for services on their behalf. They may be referred from one service-provider to another—involving different levels of government and different ministries or departments within each level of government—and have to undergo repeated assessments to get into the next agency or institution. For the chronically homeless, this can serve as another barrier to service delivery. And from the perspective of the service-providers, fragmentation is cumbersome. In times of crisis, providers may need to contact several different agencies, sorting through waiting lists, to find someone who will take their client."

This is a system that needs some serious shaking up.

I STIRRED UP SOME trouble from professional activists when I wrote a piece about my frustration and anger with a Parkdale community meeting, published in the May 28, 1998, issue of NOW magazine:

I have had a real love-hate relationship with south Parkdale since my ten years as a resident. It was where I lived and worked and fought, and the boundaries of the ward were the boundaries of my life.

It was a highly politicized community. Meetings were often the equivalent of Saturday Night Wrestling—orchestrated drama, high emotions, accusations of this and that, and attempted takeovers of the boards of local organizations by one faction or another.

We had to fight for the right to live here. Fight to keep our shabby rooming houses and boarding homes, those tiny, distressing, self-contained spaces landlords offered up for rent. Fight for recognition that this was our community too.

Tonight's meeting looks like more of the same. The city, many believe, is planning to recommend the legalization of illegal bacherlorettes—and the community is responding.

The gathering is being jointly chaired by Josie Stomp, a resident who chairs Delivery of Government Services, a quasi-official sub-committee of the city's Healthy Neighbourhoods West, and my friend Nora McCabe, of the neighbourhood committee, a body that came out of the old Community Advisory Board at the Queen Street Mental Health Centre. . . .

The room is crowded, the usual suspects in place: the rate-payers, the institution, the traditional agencies, the self-styled maverick agency, the cops, the city—and a crazy or two. Although I do try, it's hard to keep an attitude of optimism—even of detachment—for long. Accusations start off the meeting: how come I wasn't invited, how come he wasn't invited, how come, how come.

The old-style Parkdale cacophony.

Gathered here are some of the root causes of the prolonged misery that makes up the day-to-day lives of the psychiatric survivors in Parkdale. I experience a burning sense of my own culpability as I look around the room, at the agencies—the Supportive Housing Coalition, Habitat, Parc—that I had a hand in developing. And others like the Community Occupational Therapists Association, Queen Street Mental Health, Houselink, all receiving funding as a partial government response to what used to be called "the plight of the mental patient." These agencies and institutions have done well for themselves over the decades. Most have expanded their mandates, budgets and profiles. Staff, many of whom I've worked with over the years, have also done well. Community workers are now executive directors. Some have bought homes and started families, others have saved enough to be looking at moving on.

They've fared infinitely better than their clients. It's a poignant contrast, what a decade or two in the mental health world can accomplish for those paid to work within it, and what a decade or two as survivor/clients can reduce people to.

The meeting is briefly back on track. The representatives of the traditional agencies are soft-spoken, as though they might be willing to recognize culpability, though that may be a stretch. I find myself involuntarily shuddering at their eager-ness to be part of the solution. I can see the proposals now—bigger budgets, more staff, more programs that fail to address the needs of their target population. The ratepayers are stoic, resigned, although it still rankles, to being labelled the bad guys. Oddly, they are the only people, along with church representatives and the business improvement association, in the room not in some way "living off the avails of . . . "

The maverick agency representatives—self-styled Keepers of the Conscience—mistakenly believe they occupy the moral high ground, first captured fifteen years ago when I too worked there, and don't appear to be able to see themselvs as yet more publicly funded agencies in the same league and with the same failures as the others around the table. Egos, status, salaries and self-image all get in the way of reality.

The two best advocates I've ever come across, rising out of the communities they represent, both endure life-threatening diseases: AIDS and MS. They are centred, practical and, of necessity, empowering of others. They both possess an acute sense of time wasting away and of the need for many hands and voices to get things accomplished. We used to talk together about professional, or paid, advocacy and how it fostered "advocate's disease."

There is a statistically rare syndrome whose name, Munchausen by Proxy, is applied to caregivers whose charges are too often critically ill with mystifying complaints—for example, a mother whose child may be at death's door five times a year without evident cause. The parent/caregiver is addicted to the drama, the attention, the strokes, to the point of harming his or her own child. Paid advocacy, although no intentional harm is done to those advocated for, has some of the same features.

It is too easy to benevolently silence a population by speaking on behalf of it. By not examining the assumption that they are unable to speak for themselves. Too often, there are the workers' voices, the workers' solutions, leaving no room, no safe place for the disenfranchised to develop their own voice, their own capabilities. Whether we're talking about the righteous left or the demonic right, caught up in their battles and ideologies, no one is terribly interested in the uneducated, non-aligned, directly affected individual.

It's no fun to step aside, put away charts and diagrams and expertise, and trust those whom the workers do not trust.

I've learned a lot about the capabilities of my community, about leadership and its attendant responsibilities, about those who are funded to care for the vulnerable, about advocacy. I have travelled the country, been up and down the ladders of decision-making and policy formation. I've seen many other communities that are struggling to cope with rampant poverty, drug abuse and the de-institutionalized psychiatric survivors in their midst.

Here, I want to yell—what have you been doing all this time?

So many dollars are represented here. And so much failure. Twenty years of tenants' associations, twenty years of community workers, twenty years of agency development and expansion, twenty years of meetings, twenty years of change for everyone but those who need it most.

At a maximum, we're talking about 2,000 individuals living in and around Parkdale. If all the dollars supporting all the agencies and all the staff were applied directly to housing subsidies and job opportunities, rather than supportive housing and paid community workers, what could be accomplished!

City of Toronto staff will be recommending that all the players, including the owners of illegal bachelorettes, enter into a mediation process. Everyone knows that without teeth this will be useless, so another meeting will have to be held to set out the conditions for entering the process. I'd go a step further, asking the city to put out ads requesting former residents of rooming and boarding homes and bachelorettes in the area to step forward to assist directly in the process. Former because it is remotely possible, in spite of all the barriers to getting out, that some of these people will be in safe, secure housing—a necessary condition for involvement. Direct representation would eliminate the pretense of representation by workers who are in an unacknowledged conflict of interest.

It would also mean new blood, new players and, hopefully, a new immediacy.

IN TWENTY YEARS OF activism on behalf of psychiatric patients and the poor, I have seen only two positive examples of client involvement in the establishment and ongoing operation of a service. One, the Ontario Advocacy Commission, was killed in infancy by Ontario's Harris government, while the other continues its struggle against the prevailing winds.

The Gerstein Centre arose out of the Toronto Mayor's Action Task Force on Discharged Psychiatric Patients. This task force was established in 1982 in response to several boarding house deaths of ex-psychiatric patients. Its mandate was to look at what happens to people who are deinstitutionalized and to recommend solutions. It seemed unlikely that it would be able to hear and be responsive to the needs of its target group, and yet, against all odds, it was.

I've asked myself in the years since its inception what made the difference, and what made the Gerstein Centre, almost alone in my personal history of involvement in the beginnings of agencies and supports, a place that I continue to be proud to be associated with.

I can still remember the initial press conference when then-Mayor Art Eggleton announced his appointment of Dr. Reva Gerstein, a high-profile psychologist, to head up the task force. I'd been taken along by a reporter from a local television station, who rightly suspected I'd have a negative and potentially useful soundbite in reaction to this initiative.

I vividly recall staring in angry confusion at Reva, at her clothes and jewellery and generally immaculate presentation, and wondering how the hell she expected to understand and relate to those I'd left behind in my boarding home, my all-consuming world in the west end of Toronto. I was already jaded, suspicious and resentful. With good reason.

It is a useful exercise to walk into any social service agency in your own neighbourhood and to view it from the clients' perspective. While you won't find "coloured" toilets and water fountains set apart from the "white" ones, you will find a carefully replicated societal class structure, including locked staff bathrooms and open client ones. Including off-limits space, often the most desirable and attractive, reserved for staff only. Including prominently posted rules of acceptable behaviour, not for staff but for clients, that set the tone and establish generalized assumptions about the people they purport to help. *Sit quietly. Wait endlessly. Don't smoke. Don't swear. Don't ask.*

Staff are defined by their clothes, their income, their good health, good teeth, lack of urgency, by their desks and the files and the forms they keep on people like you. Clients likewise are defined by the visible characteristics of the poor—second-hand clothing, coughs and colds and the 1,001 diseases that thrive on malnutrition, the posture of defeat and failure and shame marking them as surely and clearly as skin colour.

Neither staff nor client have points of intersection outside the "therapeutic milieu." They won't shop in the same stores, live in the same neighbourhoods, have the same friends. As much as the worker will assume to know the life of her client, she sees only the 10 percent of the iceberg that is above water; the rest will remain a mystery. Concentrated primarily on crises or difficulties, it's easy after a while to reduce the clients to the problems they bring.

I was working at the Parkdale drop-in at the time, the only crazy person on staff, steeped in the day-to-day realities confronting the deinstitutionalized: shoddy and dangerous boarding and rooming houses, over-medication, substance abuse, rampant malnutrition, lice infestations, profound loneliness, and, far too often, disease and death.

And there was Reva Gerstein, appointed to do the fixing. And she did the last thing I expected. She said, "Pat, I'd like you to join my committee, to give it a strong ex-patient voice."

My skepticism notwithstanding, Reva Gerstein did what so many others in the field have failed to do: she actually listened to the members of the psychiatric community, giving as much or more weight to our perceptions of our needs as to the professionals' interpretation or spin on problems and solutions.

And this respectful listening extended to the manner in which she conducted the task force, and later the developmental board of the Centre. It was confusing for me. I was already a veteran of endless meetings with agency heads and bureaucrats, used to being dismissed, ridiculed, yelled at, even used to the stomach-churning atmosphere of being the only dissenting voice in the room, the fly in the ointment.

For a time, I figured Reva's listening and nodding must be simply another device, another tactic to get around doing anything about what I was saying. I'd get so confused, I'd go back to the drop-in scratching my head, telling Paul Quinn, then my co-worker, now director of the centre, how suspicious and disorienting I found these meetings.

"What do you think she's up to?" I'd ask him, certain I was missing something.

I sometimes think it was the first time anyone in a position to actually deliver had asked the survivor community directly what was needed, what we wanted, and her report reflected what we'd told her in public meetings.

Hospital is too scary for a lot of people—it costs too much in terms of personal autonomy and seems to rely heavily on medication as intervention. As a result, those who need help don't ask for it, sometimes even run from it. Under Reva's direction, we planned to create an environment that didn't require the handing over of self to others, that emphasized client direction, client choice and client strengths. We wouldn't be there to diagnose, or to encourage or discourage the taking of medications; our goal was to help people learn the skills to enable them to handle future crises, to provide information about resources and a safe, welcoming atmosphere.

We wanted to create a freestanding psychiatric crisis centre, not connected to a hospital, not staffed with doctors and nurses. That idea made a lot of people nervous, and our opposition was just waiting for the idea to fall apart.

Our proposal was eventually approved by the Community Mental Health branch of the provincial Ministry of Health. The board was made up initially of the task force members who wished to remain involved. Reva stayed on to chair it, and I am pleased and proud that it was my motion to name the Centre after her. Without Reva's backing, her reputation in the profession, we wouldn't have been permitted to exist. Her ultra-civilized negotiating with three separate levels of government over tea, her insistence, quiet and polite, that this was what was needed, gave much needed credibility in funding circles to an otherwise "out there" proposal.

Hiring staff—two teams of ten crisis workers—was a long, excruciating exercise. We were not looking for perfection, not seeking the Renaissance worker; we wanted people who were open to learning, who could work in partnership with the clients rather than from lofty positions of authority. Contrary to some expectations, we chose not to hire anyone whose personal views were too set to allow the client the freedom of choice we felt was integral to our philosophy.

For example, we would not hire someone who believed that meds were the only answer, and that not taking them was pure folly. Equally, we would not employ a worker who felt that all medication was bad and dangerous and shouldn't be taken. Attitude and openness, that's what we examined most closely.

The opposition were sharpening their knives—our plan was radical and thus threatening—and the antagonism was exacerbated by a board decision to give preference in hiring to those who had firsthand experience of the mental health system. Our foes believed that "client empowerment," though it looks good in mission statements and funding proposals, only gets in the way of efficient agency functioning. But there was so little hope, there were so few positive role models in our community, we were so used to being "fixed" by workers who looked nothing like us, who had none of the experience of marginalization, poverty, homelessness. We knew that had to change.

Professional resentment came in statements like: "Gerstein is paying consumers and BAS $35,000 a year." Real professionals, the logic went, should be paid more, treated better, than the new standard we'd created. It was as though they were diminished by the elevation of the para-professional, by the notion of client as worker. A kind of "there goes the neighbourhood" shudder ran through the system.

Public health nurses, a psychiatrist or two, lawyers and front-line workers from shelters and housing agencies, city officials—we were all working in harmony, not to build personal fiefdoms or reputations but to establish a new model for the delivery of care. Our front-line staff was an interesting combination of styles, backgrounds, ages, sexual preferences, race and ethnicity. So much so that it seemed at first, at least to Dr. Bob Buckingham of Toronto General Hospital, that they'd never be able to form a cohesive unit. What many did not see was the mind-set common to all these diverse people: they were willing and eager to learn, to participate in this groundbreaking effort.

Staff who work in an authoritarian atmosphere, we believed, who feel themselves powerless in the hierarchy, are reluctant to share whatever shreds of power they do have with the clients. With that in mind, we wanted to create an inclusive management style, with front-line representation on the board and its committees, not simply the director reporting on behalf of everyone else. This too was new, as most directors feel threatened by the presence around the table as equals of front-line workers, free to disagree or put forward options that might differ from those backed by the boss.

This shared decision-making started right off the bat. Staff were left to come up with their own proposal about how shifts would work, since we required a team of four people around the clock.

Paul Quinn—who'd backed and supported me and calmed me down after many confrontations with boarding home owners, politicians, civil servants and agency heads— became as interested as I was in this new phenomena: meetings where votes were rarely necessary, where discussions didn't degenerate into slanging matches, where it was assumed that if you were at the table, you had a valuable contribution to make. Paul joined up with a hospital-based social worker, Barbara Fitchette, and they applied as a team as co-directors, bringing together hospital and community experience to the position.

Decisions had to be made about who the Centre could and

could not serve, and again the wisdom of the community was listened to. There was an assumption around the board table that we could not risk having clients who were, or who said they were, suicidal. I pointed out, however, that survivors have learned that the only way to access services is to begin a conversation with "I feel like killing myself." Competition for beds was rough even back then, requiring what I call a self-destructive one-upmanship. Rather than barring those who claimed suicidal tendencies, we had to help our clients understand that this was not a requirement here. So we adopted a resolution that stated that we could not take people who were "actively" suicidal.

There was also the assumption that we wouldn't be able to help people who were so psychotic that they were unable to communicate with the workers. I got to explain that even the most seemingly "out there" conversations, if listened to carefully enough, can be understood. It would be incumbent on the worker to translate disconnected ramblings, constantly checking with the client to make sure they'd understood correctly what was being said.

The ability to self-refer, rather than be referred by a psychiatrist or social worker or other professional, was also essential and agreed to. In itself, this was a radical notion. It went against a history of access to programs involving complicated intake processes, almost always requiring professional stamps of approval.

The board also didn't want to replicate the tendency of agencies and hospitals to blacklist those who are seen as trouble-makers: any decision or effort to bar people would have to be brought to the board first for full discussion.

When it came to choosing a site for the Centre, Reva wanted to use the physical structure itself to create a new sense of entitlement and expectation for the clients: a new standard that would demonstrate to the people who used it that they deserve more than dingy shelters, dilapidated housing, roach- and mouse-infested drop-ins. And if the rest of the world picked up on this shift in attitude as well, so much the better.

A decade and a half later, sitting in the boardroom, the back door open to the parking lot, the other opening into the communal recreation space, it's almost hard to recall the months and years of planning, negotiations, disappointment, and finally the reality of our dream. The place is so substantial it could have always been here.

The Gerstein Centre is a stunningly beautiful place, in the heart of downtown Toronto, without all the usual institutional accoutrements. It's impossible to tell that it was first used as a rest-house for off-duty police officers, complete with cafeteria and hospital-style staircases. There are three parts to the Centre's service: twenty-four-hour phone lines, a mobile team that can go out and meet with clients where they'd like to be seen— where they live, or in a park or a doughnut shop—and ten beds where, by mutual agreement, clients can get some time to take a break and regain their strength. The Centre always brings to mind for me the title of Hemingway's short story: "A Clean Well-Lighted Place." Something I've longed for more than once in my life. Something too often out of reach for my peers.

The history and development of the centre parallels the history and development of the psychiatric survivor movement, and I absolutely believe that one could not have existed without the other. I got to express this to Reva at a Centre celebration this year of her elevation to the ranks of Companion of the Order of Canada.

Since its opening in 1989, the Gerstein Centre has continued to give hope to those who most need it, demonstrating how things could be. It's a place that I continue to be proud of, and which continues to support me and many other survivors.

I WAS ASKED BY the board of the Gerstein Centre in September 1989 to work with prospective board members from the ranks of psychiatric survivors. At the time we were aiming for one-third of the board to be from that community, and to create a program of sensitivity training for board members that would assist in creating an environment survivors might find welcoming.

This was for me the beginning of four years working with

the Leadership Facilitation Program, funded by the provincial government's Ministry of Health, to encourage and develop consumer leadership on an Ontario-wide basis. Assumptions about the psychiatric survivor community, its capabilities, were about to be challenged and essentially turned on their ear.

About the only decision-making that survivors had been allowed in institutions in the past was on recreational programming: where we'd go for outings, what would be served at dances. The notion that clients could serve effectively on sensitive committees like human resources and finance, that they'd therefore be aware of previously highly confidential things such as salaries and benefits, that they would actually decide who would be employed and who would not, was earthshaking, and profoundly threatening.

More traditional agencies proved highly resistant to this notion of shared power, and for a while graduates of Leadership Facilitation were subjected to agency and institution hostility, manipulation and control. I realized that to preserve our Rosa Parkeses we needed to run a parallel development with the staff of hospitals and agencies, encouraging them also to include clients in institutional decision-making. This, I hoped, would reduce resistance, and increase awareness of the positives involved in sharing power.

It was here I learned more than I ever wanted to about how the system itself, supposedly in place to assist individuals to take back control over their lives, instead guaranteed that we would continue to look towards external expertise, whether in the form of social workers or medications. How the system, by its very nature, taught those who worked within it an essential disrespect for their clients, an infantilizing of adults into dependent children, a lack of basic belief in the capabilities of the client group.

In Leadership Facilitation, we, everyone who took part, helped psychiatric survivors pick up the severed threads of their lives and get back to who they were before diagnosis, poverty, isolation and stigma defined the parameters of their world.

In small cities and towns, we'd stay for three days in a hotel, bringing up to fifteen survivors together from the surrounding region—no nurses, no shrinks, no social workers, only us. That in itself was a powerful act, a confusing and disorienting development. More than once I was told that I must be a nurse, since I had the key to the meeting room.

Men and women accustomed to little stimulation, often fighting the side-effects of their medication, began to hear each other's experiences with the system and its employees, with hospitals and incarceration.

I was a catalyst, someone much like them who could stand up and did, someone who brought good news about our capabilities, and the doors places like the Gerstein Centre had opened for us. We examined the communities in which people lived; asking questions: What is the average rent of a room or an apartment? What is it like to line up at the local food

bank? What is the transportation like? Who are the power bro-
kers in your community—the MPs, the MPPs, the mayor and
councillors? What does the local media have to say about people like you? What groups already exist (tenant associations,
legal aid, refugee groups, gay rights) that could help with
information and meeting space? What is most needed in your
community, and how can you go about providing it?

We'd role-play presentations and requests to boards of hospitals and agencies for access to space, telephones, copiers and
computers: tools essential to organizing. We explored how
agencies were funded, and who made those funding decisions.
How the Ministry of Health worked. We were putting their
world in context.

We offered expectations: a much more powerful drug than
any psychiatrist has ever prescribed. Responsibility, personal and
collective: to understand the diagnosis you were given, and why
that particular one was pasted on; the medications you took,
what were they supposed to do for you, and what they actually
did; how one's own behaviour contributes to hospitalizations,
and how to interrupt patterns of admission and re-admission.

A peer network. Peer reliance. And a job to be done, that
could be done.

We did skill audits, looking at the strengths that people
could contribute to an organizing effort—office skills, public
speaking, bookkeeping, computer knowledge that could be
taught and shared.

It was like going into dark, medieval places and turning on the lights.

SUSPECTED ARSON FIRE KILLS TWO

A fire that police believe was set deliberately claimed the lives of two people at a Parkdale rooming house and sent seven others to hospital last night.

The building, on Queen Street West near Dowling Avenue, is a halfway house for psychiatric patients.

Firefighters received a 911 call at 5:38 p.m. and rushed to the scene of a three-alarm fire—the most serious call. They rescued residents who were hanging from third storey windows and ledges.

"The scene was very intense on our arrival. They had heavy fire and smoke migrating throughout the whole building," said Toronto Fire Chief Terry Boyko.

"There was extensive heat and smoke damage throughout the top two floors. The fire went up the centre stairwell and mushroomed out from the third floor from there."

—*Sara Jean Green,*
The Globe and Mail, September 17, 1998

We're at The Raging Spoon, a restaurant staffed and run by psychiatric survivors. There is a strange mix of emotions among the people gathered here: excitement, anticipation, mourning, fear, but most of all the powerful sense of community pulling together.

The place is packed and smoky and hot. The noise level— a mixture of voices, coughing, laughter—rises steadily, creating its own music to compete with the band that plays off in a corner. It's a Friday night, and this benefit has been pulled off in fewer than seven days.

Twenty-five dollars a plate. Those who wouldn't normally be able to afford to come have been subsidized by those who sent money but won't, or can't, attend. The money will go to those who were burned out of their homes.

Diana Capponi, my sister and the co-ordinator of the Ontario Council of Alternative Businesses (OCAB), and Laurie Hall, director of A-way Express and President of the OCAB board, meet and greet and rush around taking care of last-minute details. When the firefighters arrive, a single line of uniformed men, one of them still limping and leaning on a crutch, there is a hushed, respectful silence as they are led to their place of honour.

Sitting together at another group of tables is a collection of survivors—this term taking on a very different meaning tonight—of the fatal fire at 1495 Queen Street West. It was once a building that held twelve units, apartments for people with low income. Subsequently subdivided into smaller spaces, it contained fifty-one people the night that the fire— deliberately set—took the lives of two women. Everyone here knows that without the intervention and bravery of the firefighters, the death toll would have been much higher.

The poor live in a world of impermanence and loss: it's a way of life that rarely gets any better, and often gets worse in dramatic ways. There is no such thing as the luxury of insurance, or friends and family with the space and means to take people in. Some of the people here tonight are still living on the street, one week after the conflagration. Start out with nothing, end up with less. And so it goes. But for tonight at least, there is warmth and companionship, the promise of a meal and a place to sit, and some recognition of the trials that beset them.

I'm at a table right next to the microphone, since I'm with CBC Radio reporters who are working on a documentary about Assertive Community Treatment Teams, and are intending to record the evening's speakers. My publisher, Cynthia Good, has unexpectedly shown up and joins us. It's easy to tell, at a glance, how many poor and how many of their friends and supporters are in the audience. "Dressing down," something that is frequently recommended to those with money who want to see how the other half live, is not enough to disguise health, well-being and a strong sense of self.

At least the poor have been able to come without their

workers leading them, supervising them, keeping them in line, keeping them in their place. They know this place is for them, whether or not they're officially crazy. They know, with a little opportunity, luck and room, they too could be working here, speaking here, giving here. There are no rules posted.

I had to learn, and I subsequently passed the word on to other activists, that our communities need to be constantly reminded who we are, where we come from. The moment one of us gets recognition as a leader, our own folks tend to think of that person as exceptional or educated or worse, professional. We are so unused to seeing our own potential tapped and allowed to grow that the leaders must constantly say, "What I do, what I achieve, you can do, you can achieve."

Women, blacks and gays have fought a strong and necessary battle against negative and stereotypical portrayals on television and in other media. At the root of this advocacy is an awareness of how much people need to see positive role models, heroes, people like themselves.

The poor, crazy and addicted don't have this opportunity, don't believe they possess the capability to fight for change, and so we remain at the mercy of others with their own agendas, their own lack of belief in our potential. Only here, in our own community, can we be ourselves, and find acceptance. Tolerance. Affection. Expectations.

It would be easy to let myself wallow in the despair I feel at the moment, seeing the same conditions that greeted me on arrival into this benighted community still flourishing twenty years later. But I am happy at the pride of those who've sweated in the kitchen voluntarily to make tonight's meal, at the mix of poor and healthy standing behind the serving table, smiling at each other.

I'm happy too that Nora McCabe is here with members of the Parkdale ratepayers' group, including the head of the Business Improvement Association, Mark Crowe, who was among the first to run into the burning building to try to rescue the tenants.

There is a solidarity here that is precious and so rare.

Laurie and Diana speak, mostly about the firefighters, and they are constantly interrupted by clapping and cheers. The group of men look alternately sheepish, gratified and deeply touched at the gratitude displayed.

I hear both speakers say how rare it is to have a professional come to their rescue. Diana, who the Queen Street Mental Health Centre happily discharged to the same boarding home I lived in, talked about how worried she was, down in a basement room, about fire, and how strongly she felt that if it happened, no one would come. Laurie and Diana say, to an appreciative, knowing laugh, how in our community we mostly see these firefighters when they are peeling us off the pavement, when sunstroke or too much booze or whatever causes the collapse.

These people risked their lives for us, lives we'd never thought anybody would risk anything for.

I am supposed to read tonight, from *Upstairs in the Crazy House*, my first book, about the psychiatric boarding house in Parkdale where I was sent from hospital to live in 1978. I intend to read the chapter about an incident of arson that took place there, and about the odd young man who started it. I am very comfortable with speaking, a little less so with reading, especially within my own community, but halfway through my story my throat absolutely closes down, and I can't get a word out without choking. The thought of failing to finish, to do what I'd been asked to do on this of all nights, causes a brief flash of panic until I remember Cynthia's presence. A touch on her shoulder is enough to convey the need, and without a pause she continues reading in a clear and passionate voice. An unintended but inspired gift to the community. It's nice to have people who can be depended on.

People from the house are asked if they would like to say anything, about their experiences, about tonight. The first to speak is a large, shy woman, whom the audience encourages to come forward. She explains, trembling a little at the mike, that she is not a psychiatric survivor but someone who experienced years of abuse. She says her family and friends gradually moved away as she grew into adulthood, and that she'd taken this room as the first step in creating a world of her own.

"Now someone had the nerve to take away my house, my possessions. Someone took something away from me—my home." She's on the street, too familiar a place.

After her comes an odd-looking person with a badly swollen face, introduced as Tiffany. She talks about thirty years as a psychiatric consumer. How she's been through every form of abuse, including this latest episode that required her to go for reconstructive surgery on her jaw. She gets beaten up a lot, having started life as a man, trying to live it now as a woman, apparently viewed as too unstable for the gender-switch program offered through the Clarke Institute.

"I know what it's like to lose everything. And now again. Thanks to the two firefighters only two people died. I was thinking of going to sleep there that night. I could have died too."

A good-looking but "out there" young man is next. He's still in shock, and it is effectively conveyed when he falters, staring straight ahead, seeing: "There's two of us that died, two of us very dead. That first night, after seeing people in body bags, people lying there dead . . . I'm very happy to be here with my friends tonight, very happy to see you all. The building is charcoal. We're here. I'd like to have a moment of silence. For them. Hell, I'm not crazy, but this could drive us crazy. A moment of silence?"

From Tiffany: "Yes, I was going to suggest that."

And we are silent as the young man, tears in his eyes, goes and stands near the open back exit door.

After the uncomfortable silence, Tiffany steps forward and says, "Why don't we say something together? The Lord's

Prayer, how about we say that together?" She leads the group, sometimes mumbling words she doesn't know or remember, and the audience follows.

"Our Father Who art in Heaven . . . "

A few days later, still in the mild euphoria lingering from the success of that night, the people at The Raging Spoon are distraught to learn that Tiffany has been arrested and charged with arson and murder. They know too well how this will be portrayed in the news media, "like Charles Manson delivering the eulogy for his victims."

And indeed, her swollen face contributes to the perfect portrait of a societal nightmare: the psychiatric patient. She is variously portrayed as a transvestite, a person with fourteen personalities, a mental patient, a tenant of the building.

In the community, she's long been known as a deeply screwed-up person, very needy and often alone.

At the Spoon, there is an air of defeat, anticipating all the "Lock them up and medicate them" letters and articles to come. I get a call asking my advice on how to handle the media through the onslaught.

"No comment on the arrest, lots to say on housing conditions," I suggest.

This confirms the questioner's own thoughts but does nothing to dissipate the gloom, the sense of all that is arrayed against them.

THURSDAY, OCTOBER 8, 1998, the *Toronto Star* carried a bold, bleak headline on its front page, above the fold:

PLIGHT OF THE HOMELESS A "NATIONAL DISASTER"

So is the plight of those who never stood a chance.

I'm talking to a seventeen-year-old single mother. Her name is June, and the infant she holds is a few months old. When June herself was born, both her parents were heroin addicts. June's mom Claire was horribly abused most of her early life, resulting in feelings of worthlessness and inadequacy that haunted her for years. The only time she ever felt at peace within herself was when she was on the needle. June's father was from a very privileged background, the only son of wealthy parents who overindulged him, and tried unsuccessfully to buy him out of his habit.

When June was a few months old, her mom, for the sake of her child, wrenched herself out of the life and stayed out. It was a herculean accomplishment, done without benefit of medications or therapies, which she'd tried from time to time and found irrelevant. It was a feat that her former partner could not or would not emulate.

Claire's extended family was equally messed up; early pregnancies, addictions and abusive relationships seemed the norm. Interventions that might have been successful with her parents (for that matter her parents' parents) weren't tried.

There were no Children's Aid workers or marriage counsellors or even a societal recognition that husbands shouldn't beat their wives and kids.

Claire got into trouble at school early, her lack of any positive self-image had her seeking relations with other "bad kids," and there was no effort on the part of teachers or principals to deal with what was clearly a kid thrashing about looking for help. She left school, believing her father right that she was too stupid to benefit from finishing her education, and went out into the world of work.

Claire was so uncomfortable in her own body and around others at her various workplaces that she'd eat lunch in a bathroom stall, rather than try to socialize and set herself up for further rejection or ridicule.

It was on a trip to India that she first tried heroin, and when she came back to Canada it was what—oddly—kept her alive for the next decade or so, keeping the desperate pain at bay.

On Ontario's Family Benefits program, she went back to school and found herself making grades she'd never believed herself capable of achieving. She slowly got into advocacy, and found herself with positive role models who could help by providing a context for her suffering and an safe outlet for her rarely voiced ambitions, wants and needs.

June was an outgoing child, spontaneous and curious and fearless and smart. Early on, though, she was very aware that other children had fathers, and where was hers and why wasn't he there? You can't explain to a child that her daddy is an addict, in and out of jail, and that at this stage of her life she's better off without him.

Life got especially difficult during June's early adolescence, understandably yet unavoidably. Claire had a right to some kind of life and partner, and by choice or nature Claire began long-term lesbian relationships.

"I hated her partner, I hated her being gay," June says. "I used to hide the pictures my mother had of her hanging on the walls before my friends came over." Counselling didn't help her.

They lived in a poor area of Toronto, because for a long time they were poor, and that meant attitudes weren't really progressive among June's friends. It's acceptable to have a father in jail, but not to have a mother who's gay.

Not surprisingly, June started skipping school, hanging out with boys, being sexually active. She had a lot of friends. "They were all different kids, you couldn't say they were all one type. They smoked and stuff, they thought going to jail would be cool, but they still did their homework, they weren't bad kids. I was a good student too, on paper. I got along with my teachers, at least till I started not doing my homework, and skipping."

There was an argument, too common these days, over a boy. The two girls got into a shoving match, then a fight, during which June threw a pencil at her rival.

"Other students were taking sides, you know? There were

almost a dozen kids in my class who kept it going, because it was exciting . . . I'd walk by a group of kids, and they'd be whispering, and I didn't mind. I didn't know their names, but they knew who I was, and that felt good."

A few weeks after the event, with the encouragement of a vice-principal, the girl laid charges. June was charged (because of the pencil) with assault with a deadly weapon and told not to come back to school. This of course meant more time to get into situations that were unhealthy and illegal. Her mother worked days and some evenings, and the atmosphere at home grew tense. June resisted attending an alternate school set up in the local mall.

Lifting the baby to her breast for feeding, June sighs. "I can't believe I did all those things. That it was me. We had stolen credit cards and we bought all kinds of clothes and jewellery. We even rented limos to take us to bars and shopping malls downtown."

"You must have known you'd get caught?"

"No, I honestly didn't. I thought we'd sneak the credit cards back into her [friend's mother's] purse, and that they wouldn't know it was us. I know, I know how stupid that sounds. And it wasn't like I was this hard-done-by poor kid with no clothes. I like clothes a lot. If I saw a jacket, say a $200 Tommy Hilfiger jacket, and right beside it one that was exactly the same except for the label, for $150, I'd buy the Hilfiger one."

"So tell me why."

"It's like a step up, you know? People look at you and they don't think you're struggling. You know everyone wants one, and you're the one who's wearing it. Everyone my age and younger feels that. Hell, I know a mother with an eight-year-old who keeps telling her he needs a Ralph Lauren jacket."

It couldn't and didn't last. When she was arrested, her mother had to bring clothing to her in jail, since everything she was wearing was stolen.

She was sentenced to four months in an open custody setting, though to call it "open" is a bit misleading. It was away from the city, and if she wanted to call her friends she first had to submit their names (with their permission) for a criminal record check. She liked some of it—the counsellor and some of the other girls—resented other parts, but on the whole, looking back, she's decided it was good for her.

She has three weeks to find a new place to live. The co-op where she grew up has rejected her as a tenant, claiming that she should have known that, as soon as she turned sixteen, she was required to attend co-op meetings regularly. Acceptance there would have meant security, since rent is geared to income, and would also have enabled her to remain in a neighbourhood she knows. Her options in Toronto's housing market, where landlords have waiting lists and choices, are next to none.

The maximum shelter allowance she's entitled to is $511, with a payment on top of that of $450 for living expenses. Under Ontario's new rules, she will have to actually move into her own place before family benefits will kick in for the new rent, and they no longer pay the last month's deposit that all landlords demand.

It's hard for her to get around on the transit system. She has a large, heavy carriage that can't safely make it down escalators; carrying the baby for any length of time, along with diapers, strains her back and arms.

The baby is fat and content, gurgling and smiling. She wanted to have him circumcised but provincial health insurance doesn't cover that any more, she tells me matter-of-factly.

For a time, she attended a program for teenage pregnant mothers. Some of what she saw and learned there was useful; other things just seemed silly.

"It was very crowded, there were more pregnant girls than chairs, so you'd have to stand or lean against the wall. They'd help you plan and create a meal, but everyone would work on parts of the same one, so you'd have four girls in charge of grating cheese. Two minutes of that, and you're back to waiting. I liked the others, but there's only so much you can talk about, you know?"

She is a disarming combination of adult and child; depending on the topic she switches back and forth.

"I wrote to my baby, after he was born, seven pages. I told him about the pregnancy, how I hated being pregnant, but how I loved to feel him kick inside me. I told him how loved he would be. How a whole bunch of people already loved him.

That he's going to be an only child because giving birth is really painful. How I was told he'd probably be ugly when he was born, because most newborns are, but how beautiful he was, how chubby his cheeks were, and how he even had a double chin, and just a bit of a conehead. I told him how I lay awake watching him that first night, for fear he'd stop breathing. I want him to know that I won't be a welfare mother, that I'm going to go back to school, make something of myself. I know it will be hard, but my mother did it."

These days are different.

> Special needs funding for the following have been cut in various provinces: diabetic supplies, food vouchers, transportation allowances for seeking work or going to a job, winter clothing allowances, baby formula and other necessary items for children, school supplies, costs related to a training program, preventive dental care, deposits for utility hookups, assistance for vehicle repairs in rural areas, utility bills and rents in arrears.
>
> —*NAPO press release, April 15, 1997*

The odds against children born into poverty making it out are increasing exponentially. No one and everyone is responsible for ensuring that these children have a chance.

CHAPTER FIVE

Montreal

Rue St. Denis

ALTHOUGH I WAS BORN in Montreal and spent the first ten years of my life in the inner city—playing ball, cards and marbles in streets and alleyways—my family soon joined the exodus to the suburbs, first to the underdeveloped area of St. Eustache Sur-le-Lac (now called Deux Montagnes) and then to Chomedy, Laval. Travel to the downtown was reserved for Christmas shopping excursions—Eaton's and Simpson's in particular. As I got older, taking the train into the city became synonymous with escaping the violence at home, and pulling into Central Station always felt like the beginning of a great adventure.

When I was accepted into the Creative Arts program at Dawson College, the first English CEGEP in Montreal, real life—and real freedom—began for me . . . despite the fact that I'd already spent five months on a psychiatric ward. Maybe that's why I feel exhilarated to come back, even though I know that this is not going to be any kind of holiday.

For the purposes of objective research, I wanted to find a place to stay in an area of the Montreal that I'm unfamiliar with, to help me get a new look at the city. I went online to find a bed and breakfast and came up with one that promised it was both central and cheap—important criteria to a writer on a limited expense budget. I was pretty pleased with myself.

The plane ride, only an hour, passed in its usual medicated blur, and soon I'm in a cab heading towards the B&B where I'll be based for a week. I know something's off as soon as the driver pulls up in front. It doesn't look anything like the picture that was displayed on the website. Of course, it didn't occur to me that there might be more than one establishment with the same name on the same street, subtly differentiated by subtitles that I'd missed.

I struggle with my bags up the front steps, and there is no helpful doorman, not even an open door. I look around in a slight panic and see an intercom arrangement. I buzz, and after a moment, with no voice contact, I'm buzzed in.

The lobby, such as it is, does nothing to bolster my confidence. It's at the bottom of a long staircase, flanked on one side by pop and snack machines. A fellow sits in an easy chair behind the front desk, watching television. My arrival must have coincided with a commercial, because he's up and smiling at me. I identify myself, and his smile broadens. Clearly, I'm some kind of event—staying a whole week, pre-paid with my publisher's American Express card.

I get only one key, the one to my room, up on the second floor. For security reasons, there is no front-door key; someone is always on duty to buzz residents in. I'm already thinking this is going to be a very long week.

I struggle with my bags up the narrow staircase, then proceed gingerly down a dim corridor with a number of closed doors till I reach the one with my assigned number, close to the end. I put the key in the door and try to gather my resources for the assault I fear awaits me.

Deep breath, turn the key, open the door, reach in without looking, run a hand along the wall till it hits a switch and a light comes on. Wait some more. A lesson learned the hard way: give plenty of time for anything that scampers or slithers or crawls to run for cover.

"Chickenshit," I mutter to myself, and barge my way in, leading with my large knapsack and dropping both bags at my feet. I know I was aiming for economy, but this is one step beyond. Not certain what I'm going to do, I light a cigarette and convince myself that I should at least explore just how bad it is.

High ceiling. That's a plus. A television to the left of the door, up high near the ceiling, on a platform, as if it were a hospital room. A sink, clean. A mirror over it. A soap dish in between. Looking closely, I see a bunch of bristles and grunge under the small, wrapped bar of face soap.

I bang, wait, then open the cupboard below the sink, wincing. What I decide is mouse poison (because I don't want to believe it's rat bait) has been scattered around a plastic dish.

The bed is odd. It's been made with hospital-corner precision, yet the bottom mattress is naked and torn, the stuffing spilling out. It's thinner, longer and wider than it should be, more like a platform than a bed. I don't try it yet. I fold back the cover, which is thin and worn; the sheets are clean. I stop short of pulling back the sheets. Two pillows. I don't look inside the pillowcases, either.

A tiny bar fridge like the one I have at home, jammed under some shelves that go darkly back to the wall. Mental note: put nothing on these shelves. *If* I stay.

A small clothes cupboard with a few dangling wire hangers. There is (I say a prayer of thanks) a bathroom. Clean toilet, one of those showers installed all in one piece. Two thin, white, woefully inadequate hand towels hang from a rack.

I back out, walk to the window. It's a nice big one, but there's a sticker warning that it's alarmed and if I open it, it will scream at me. Closer examination shows that the wires that should be in contact are in fact not, so I slide it open and breathe fresh air. I see the typical, trademark Montreal black metal fire-escape stairs leading conveniently right to my window from the parking lot downstairs.

A loose chair near the window: a refugee from a kitchen suite? A night table of sorts. No convenient place to put it, so it stands a little in front of the fridge, and almost within reach of what will be for me (if I stay) the head of the bed. On the table is one of those ineffectual, cheap lamps sporting three small Christmas tree bulbs. Screwed into the table is a holder for the remote, which I remove, and turn on the television. That works okay, and clearly it has cable. Overcrowding the table is an old black phone: I lift the mouthpiece off the cradle and hold it suspiciously to my ear, relieved that there's a dial tone.

My middle-aged eyes require more light for reading than is cast from the ceiling bulbs, so I look for a way to turn on the lamp. At first I think either I've got one of those clap-on, clap-off ones or loose wiring, because when I touch it to look for the switch, on it comes. A feeble glow. There is a shelf over the bed, recently dusted.

And the walls? Well, the one I'll be looking at, if I ever actually sit on the bed, is done in the "basement rec-room in the suburbs" style of fake wood panelling, including fake wood knots (and the occasional real hole).

There's a thermostat on the wall, and I turn it to 65 degrees, while wondering if—like the window alarm—it's disconnected, and has been left around for show.

Through all this, though I pretend I'm reserving judgment, I'm really talking myself down: "Not so bad, really. You've been in a lot worse. Haven't seen a bug."

Still, I'm worried.

I'm worried what kinds of noises will be heard from the corridor as night falls. I'm worried that I didn't bring any sweat pants; I don't want to lie in that bed with any bare skin showing. I'm worried that, believing I would be in a more or less equipped hotel, I didn't bring real towels.

Gingerly, I lower myself onto the bed and try to prop myself up in a sitting position with the two flat pillows I've been allotted. Not comfortable but not terrible. I compromise. Unpack my books, my notepads and pens. The remainder mostly stays in the knapsack. Zipped up against intruders. Little, tiny potential intruders.

I'm reminded of all the rooms I've ever stayed in through my life—including some very peculiar ones strung out along what was then Dorchester Boulevard, now renamed René Lévesque Boulevard.

I've always been aware of the powerlessness and dependence that seems to crash down on the head of anyone entering a psychiatric institution; this room provokes the same reaction. It involves being put in your place, a negative affirmation about your position in the scheme of things, a dependence on the goodwill—not the legal obligations—of whoever is renting to you. An awareness that the laws and by-laws put in place to govern these spaces are never based in reality, that the cost of trying to invoke them can be eviction, or worse, physical retribution. How bad is the landlord? How critical are the corners he chooses to cut? How much of a firetrap is the building? Who else does he rent to? If standards are too high—demands for references, credit reports, first and last months' rent—odds are you won't get in. If there are no standards, if he rents to anyone, then safety becomes even more of a factor.

In the rooms I lived in here in downtown Montreal, while I was a college student, I met my first drug dealers, my first hookers and thieves, the defeated and the drunks and the delusional. One place—a tiny, tiny place with a crash-bar door leading to an external staircase, it was actually an expanded fire exit—I got for free as long as I agreed to type up the details of an eye operation the superintendent of the building claimed to have perfected, to bring back the sight of the blind. Of course, he also assured me that the FBI and the CIA had the building surrounded to prevent details of his operation falling into the wrong hands. I stayed for a few months and typed up his scrawled, incomprehensible notes, till my worries about his "experiments" and his "subjects" and his paranoia became overwhelming.

I got used to fending off unsolicited advances in the hallways, stepping over the collapsed bodies of drunks who couldn't make it all the way up the stairs, and especially learned to avoid the shared kitchen area and its infestations. I also got used to believing *this is how things are when you have little or no money.* I never got used to sharing the bathrooms. Now, of course, now that even these kinds of rooms have grown too expensive for the bottom tier of the population, I could get nostalgic for a time when there was sufficient indoor space for the impoverished to occupy.

At two in the morning I'm still awake, tossing and turning and listening to the bed protest with arthritic squeals. I've left the lamp on; it serves as a feeble night light. It's 2 degrees outside, and probably 10 degrees in this room. This first-night wakefulness is especially familiar: what noises will the darkness produce? What will crawl or skitter out of holes in the baseboards, or out of the mattress itself? What will I do if I hear the doorknob turn?

I'm remembering, too, the first eighteen years of my life, of being in a bedroom that was no guarantee of safety or security or even privacy, how very real and immediate was the threat of the door crashing open, of being dragged out of sleep for a beating, whatever time of night or day, never quite knowing what the crime was.

But it's quiet, except for the television, a sound I take advantage of to mask any other noise, a sound I use to comfort myself, remind myself that there is a larger world, a normal world of expectations and happenings and promise.

I fall asleep at some point, a restless and eerie half-sleep that leaves me exhausted in the morning.

> MONTREAL'S DIRECTOR OF PUBLIC health says many citizens in Canada's third-largest city are literally sick of being poor. The city currently has an unemployment rate of almost 12% and nearly 25% of its families live below the poverty line....
>
> The annual report from the Regional Council for Health and Social Services for the island of Montreal indicates that poor Montrealers can expect to live 5 fewer years than those with higher incomes. Other findings are not surprising: more low-income earners smoke, infant-mortality rates are higher and the birth rate is 6 times higher among adolescents living in low-income parts of the city.
>
> —*Website, Canadian Medical Association Journal, 1998*

THE NEXT MORNING, EARLY, I discover the "breakfast" part of the B&B. The guy behind the counter stops me as I'm heading to the doughnut shop across the street.

"Wait, I'll give you coffee." He nukes a stale croissant and pours a small cup of foul-tasting brew. Not a great start to the day.

Heading out, it's like stepping out of a cave into daylight, though the day itself is grey and cold and unwelcoming. I visit the bus terminal a few streets away, watch the comings and goings, trying to shake a mood that hangs around me all day.

Later on, I brave the subway system. I'm startled by how packed it is, when it's not even rush hour. My first thought, watching how closely people stand at the edge of the platform, is that these commuters clearly haven't heard of the subway shovings by a few people labelled "mentally ill" in Toronto. I visualize someone running up and down screaming: The schizophrenics are coming! The schizophrenics are coming!

I manage to get into a car, jammed up against an angry-looking young man. His anger is not directed at me, apparently, for which I'm relieved. Shaking his head in disbelief at the crowding and discomfort, he starts talking to me in French, then switches to English when I look at him quizzically.

"It's stupid," he says, with a foreshortened wave around him. "Montreal has too many people, that's all. They should take out the seats, they take up too much room."

He's right: later on, when I'm able to sit, I find my knees and that of the person sitting opposite pretty much touching, and obstructing the aisle.

I visit some of the stores and restaurants I used to frequent downtown. Everything seems pretty much deserted, and the service is dispirited. Just walking aimlessly, I find areas downtown that make me nervous. This is new to me, this sense of danger: of men who have nothing to do; of women burdened with children and no life.

My room is less depressing than the downtown, and I go back there.

I FIND MYSELF BARELY able to function the rest of my stay. I can't shake the depression and sense of loss I'm feeling. I want to yell at the crowds of heads-down people: "What did you do to yourselves?!"

I sit on the stairs, waiting for Stan and Sharon Asher to pick me up. When I'd phoned to say I was coming to Montreal, they were excited and pleased. So was I. It was very considerate of them, I said, to have kept the same phone number and resided in the same house all these years.

Although both now teach at John Abbot College, Stan was my former (North American literature) high school teacher. I probably presented him with the challenge of a lifetime. Theirs was the only family I'd ever met, back when I was disintegrating into the first of numerous mental breakdowns, in which the children were happy, and nobody ran and hid when Daddy came home. You could actually feel the love, humour and deep affection that formed the basis of their marriage.

In the same way that Freda learned there was such a thing as social drinking from white, middle-class society, the Ashers taught me, just by being themselves, how families were meant to be.

When Sharon gave birth to her third child, they asked me to work for them during the summer. They might not have known, but it got me away from my house at a time when I really needed to be elsewhere. I spent the summer playing with babies and toddlers, and listening to Sharon laugh as she tried to cope with her little brood. There was no hitting, not even any yelling, when one of the children spilled something, or crayoned on a wall. The children were meant to be enjoyed, little gifts from God in diapers and undershirts.

Trying to keep them occupied and happy taught me how to play. And all the while, Sharon would heap praise on me, telling me I was saving her sanity. Like I was doing them a favour.

I hated going home, where there was no safe place, where everything only got worse in a way that bred nightmares. I couldn't talk about that to anyone; nor could I discuss the strangeness of the differences between the two places: night and day.

I was different as well. Although I didn't believe Sharon when she told me how wonderful I was, it was the first time in my young life—I was fifteen or sixteen years old—that I'd heard anything positive about who I was, or what I did. From her, and from Stan, who valued my writing enough to have me read on his university radio show, I was getting another picture of myself.

At home, it was purely a matter of survival. Of getting through long nights without being beaten, or having to witness my mother or siblings getting knocked around. Of tiptoeing around the monster on the couch, of trying—and constantly failing—not to screw up, not to add to the thick tension in the house. Of trying to be invisible.

I had no idea what that environment was doing, had done, to my perception of myself, and, by extension, my perception of the world. It was easier to believe that horror resided in every house, just behind the façade of suburban tidiness and contentment. Everyone went to bed in fear, woke up in fear, breathed it, ate it, drank it. And everyone hid it, lied about it, constructed pleasant little fairy tales of family life.

If you're not loved as an infant, as a child, as a teenager, it has to be your fault. If there's violence, you must have done something to deserve it. You're told that so often, it must be true.

Sitting on the stairs, lost in memories, my knapsack beside me, I'm startled by someone calling my name. Standing there, totally out of context, is a woman I know from Toronto, a nurse who has served on various committees with me. She's looking piercingly at me, then up at the building where I'm staying, and I can tell she's doing an informal mental health assessment.

"Pat, what are you doing here?"

"You first," I grin at her.

She's been visiting her son, who lives a few streets away. It's her last day here, she'll be driving back home this afternoon.

I explain about doing research for my book, and I watch her struggle with herself over whether to believe me or to intervene in my best interests. I exude enough reassurance to get her back in her car, and resume my waiting. When the Ashers pull up, I pile into the back of their van.

It's like entering a time warp—a warm, comfortable feeling of affection given and returned. They are, like me, a little older, a little greyer. But, as we drive around the city streets that used to be so alive, so vibrant, so teeming with possibilities, it's clear that the Montreal that shaped us is gone.

Now the feeling surrounding the trudging, worried pedestrians is the same self-absorption, the same weight of unrelieved worry and affliction, that marks GO Train passengers at rush hour in Toronto. St. Catherine Street, one of the best downtown streets in Canada, is only a shadow of what it was. The areas I know best, from Atwater to Central Station, are unrecognizable. Homeless mentally ill panhandle where the Montreal Forum used to be. "For Sale" signs replace businesses. Women don't like to walk this stretch at night, this territory that we used to play in as students after midnight.

Stan says that when he gets together with friends and rela-
tives at bar mitzvahs, weddings or funerals, the first question
people put to one another is: "And where are your children
now?" His three kids, the children I babysat a lifetime ago, are
all living in Toronto.

The neighbourhoods edging on the downtown don't look
poor from the outside. The buildings, the old ones, are attractive, and it's possible to miss the fact, if it's not pointed out to
you, that inside them people are hungry.

There was no better place than Montreal in the late 1960s
and 1970s for political activists to learn their trade. An hon-
ourable trade. Every one seemed to have an idea, an opinion,
and a willingness to express it, argue over it, even fight for it.
Anything seemed possible.

There was also a huge pride in the city and the province,
and in the political and intellectual leaders we had, foremost
among them René Lévesque and Pierre Trudeau. Our writers
and poets were winning worldwide recognition—and our
hockey team was unquestionably the best! We'd hosted a very
successful world's fair, and we felt that we'd rightly taken our
place on the world stage.

Although we were English-speaking, at the time, students
like me felt that we would be part of the new country of
Quebec when it finally came about—that we'd have a chance
to do things right, have real social justice. I remember one
afternoon, during the FLQ crisis, I was in a tiny room working

at my desk on an old typewriter when a loud boom that shuddered the desk and knocked things to the floor made my heart jump. Less than five minutes later, a friend of mine raced up the fire escape to my window, yelling, "It's started! The revolution's here! We have to get guns!"

Okay, so we were naïve.

Another mailbox had exploded, and since we lived near the street that divided Westmount, the upscale enclave of the English, from St. Henri, the land of the poor, we felt it.

Now the politics of division are at work. The English discovered the importance of language rights, and the French the joy of getting your own back. Referendum anxiety built. Business pulled out, and so did jobs, optimism, opportunity and an overall sense of well-being.

As we drive through St. Henri and Verdun, I remember how even the anti-poverty groups back in the '70s operated with such a degree of enthusiasm and panache that they acted like a magnet, attracting large numbers of volunteers and helping hands. That, too, is a thing of the past.

What we've lost, I think, is that feeling that we can take the present, and the future, into our own hands.

LEADERSHIP IN THE UNDERCLASS is perhaps the most challenging kind of activism. Communication between activists across the country is incredibly difficult, since phones are often

a luxury and long-distance calls far too expensive to be a possibility. Fax machines are the property of funded agencies, not
of individuals on welfare. The cost of stamps and envelopes,
the cost of reproducing documents to send out, the transportation costs to get people to meetings, are all prohibitive.

There is often no safe base to organize from, the activist
himself being constantly bombarded by the consequences of
prolonged poverty: ill health, hunger, fear of eviction, and that
generalized moment-to-moment fearful awareness that things
can always get worse. Activists themselves become divided up,
the same way we divide up the assistance offered, and get
trapped and isolated in their own little worlds. The big picture
becomes elusive, connections don't get made.

The building housing this anti-poverty group in Notre-
Dame-de-Grâce (NDG) is empty except for three people. The
donations of clothing smell of mould.

"If we give up, there will be no dissenting voice," says
Annette, who runs this operation. "That's what happened in
Nazi Germany, no dissenting voices. We are the ones, in various progressive movements, who say: this is wrong, this isn't
true. We're on a train hurtling towards an abyss. It's only if
there are enough people standing in front of the train, building an alternative track, that we might all be saved. Otherwise,
humanity is doomed."

Those who choose to act as champions of the poor and disenfranchised are themselves trapped and demoralized: by the

enormity of the problems, the lack of solutions, and, for people like Annette, now fifty-three years old, by poverty itself.

Annette has lived on the fringes of society most of her adult life. Born in England, she grew up in Norway. She still remembers the lingering effects of war, the presence of unexploded bombs in the back yards of neat little houses.

Her parents travelled a lot, and she went from Norway to Holland, to Newfoundland, then Montreal. "Before I even reached adolescence," she says, "I'd lived in four different countries."

Her father worked in aviation, as a mechanic. He was originally from a small island in Norway, and he served in the merchant marine and the military. Annette describes her mother as a "victim of the patriarchy, male domination and privilege." Her parents divorced when she was seventeen, a good thing for both of them, she feels.

What does she have, if anything, to look forward to?

"I made it this far, so if I get to fifty-five, I'll be moved from welfare onto pension. I'll be better off. You receive $712 if you live alone."

"Not much of a goal," I say softly. "Do you ever wish things had turned out differently for you?"

"Sure, I have regrets. I've worked really hard, and there's never anything comes out of it, not for me personally. I guess I've gone through two-thirds of my life, I've experienced rage, anger and despair: it's all still there in some respects. I'm not even sure I've been able to effect immediate change, or if I'll see the effects of the efforts of people like me in my lifetime. I think the first time I became politically aware was during the Cuban missile crisis, you know, the sirens going off all the time. I realized then that the people who are in control of this planet are insane."

Poison pools at the bottom, where the ladder turns into a chute, slick and without footholds. Diseases like AIDS, tuberculosis and Hepatitis C; drugs—new and old—ranging from smack to crack; prostitution—foulness spreads in ever-widening circles.

Things are coming unglued. Where once we stepped over one drunk passed out and snoring on the sidewalk, we now step over children huddled in sleeping bags: angry, defiant, dangerous children we refuse to recognize as our own. They seem to gather in clumps at Metro stations, packs of kids in leather and denim, hair shorn or up in spikes. They all have a patina of road dust and dirt, and an aura of danger. There is no one able or willing to speak to me in English, and, of course, being raised in Montreal and "learning French" in every grade, I have no command of the language.

According to the executive director of Dans La Rue, a shelter, drop-in and medical facility dedicated to street kids, the children who can speak English just keep running, out to places like Vancouver. The rest are trapped here. "Pops," a.k.a. Father Emmett Johns, the founder of Dans La Rue, is responsible for the Metro station gatherings. Almost a decade ago, he started handing out hot dogs to street kids. In 1997, 40,000 hot dogs were distributed from a van belonging to the organization to the children in the streets, making the first "helping connection" the kids have seen for a while.

The staff at Dans La Rue, on Ontario Street East, see children as young as twelve and up to twenty-five. Most have run away from small towns outside of the city, escaping physical or sexual abuse in their families, for life on the street. Here, they fall prey to street drugs, prostitution and crime. Staff try a variety of ways to snag the children, hot dogs being the least complicated. There's education upgrading available, nursing care, a food and clothing distribution area, even a place with large metal rings drilled into the concrete floor, for the children to tie up the "drug dogs" that are their frequent companions, protecting dealers from ripoffs and stalling police.

In 1996, Dans La Rue handled 30,000 visits to the van, received 15,612 daytime visits at the emergency shelter, helped 740 kids find housing, another 573 fight drug addiction, 452 children return to their families, and provided help and friends/mentors to 567 street kids looking for work. As well, 28,000 bags of groceries were distributed.

This whole organization grew out of Pops's efforts, including the Bunker, a shelter that can house twenty kids a night. They have an arrangement with the people responsible for children's services, a postponing of the legal requirement to report underage children for three days, which means the kids can have short vacations from the street without being hauled away. There are few rules here, aside from respecting people and property.

While I'm in Montreal, they are preparing for a fundraising dinner that Mila Mulroney is backing. I raise my eyebrows under my hat when I see the television promo, since I'm not her biggest fan, but I keep my opinions to myself.

It's crowded and noisy in the Ontario Street offices. A makeshift band is practising head-banger music. A nurse is talking to a young woman while examining her feet. The donations room is spilling over with sanitary napkins, boxes of Kraft Dinner, tinned goods and a variety of clothing.

It's difficult, walking through here, feeling the hostility radiating from some of the drop-ins, not to see this as the devolution of our societal efforts at child rescue. I flash back to the orderly, middle-class group home environment of Couvrette House, the home I ran for Summerhill Homes here in the city, in which seven teenage boys were given another chance at life.

It's nice for Mila of course, and her efforts at rehabilitating her public image as a caring, maternal person. It's even nice for the staff and volunteers who are engaged in worthwhile efforts. But—it's so little, and so late.

SARAH WAS BORN IN St. John's, Newfoundland.

She left home in 1993 to study modern dance at the Toronto Dance Theatre for four years, five days a week, from eight in the morning to five at night. Sarah had student loans to enable her to live and learn. After graduation, she picked up work waitressing on trendy Queen Street until, on April 21, 1997, she was hit by a Jeep Cherokee while on her bike, breaking her elbow and banging up her knees.

A waitress isn't much use with one arm in a cast, she was $20,000 in debt to the government for the student loans now due, and she was unable even to audition for dancing roles.

"I had to deal with the driver's insurance company—they base what they pay out on the income lost. They took my basic, part-time waitressing salary, not factoring in tips or the fact that I couldn't dance, as the amount of income lost. I tried getting a lawyer, expensive when there's no money, but basically I was told there was nothing they could do. It's wild how all these things happen: you get the feeling the universe is trying to tell you something."

She applied for Employment Insurance, because the insurance payout was dragging on so long, but of course, that also takes a lot of time to kick in, so she found herself in a welfare office.

"I freaked on them. I'm sitting there, my arm in a cast, I've explained to them what was happening, all the waiting, and I was refused. They told me I had to prove I'd tried every other option. It was a pretty nasty experience."

Her rent was $500 a month.

"I was so angry and so sad. I couldn't believe welfare wouldn't help me through this, I mean, what else is it for if not for emergencies like this, the social safety net?"

She managed to find roommates who could cover the rent. The place was small and it got "pretty squishy."

She went back every day for a week: "I kept crying in front of him, appealing for reason—you have to help me! He understood, he let me sit at his desk and cry, but he said he was very sorry, he was a government employee and had to follow the guidelines. I was twenty-two at the time, a productive person trying my very best. Not everyone is a lazy good-for-nothing trying to take advantage of the government."

By August, she was able to dance again, landing gigs in Toronto, and in September it seemed the stars were aligned in her favour. Months before, she'd filled out an application for a Canada Council grant to further her dance studies in Montreal. Now she was given $8,000 to cover her expenses for three months. She wasn't unhappy to leave Toronto.

This money was to cover rent and food and classes, which ranged from $7 to $10 a session, as well as special workshops, which cost between $200 and $300. Montreal hosts a Festival of New Dance every two years, and that took a chunk for a pass.

"I took every class I could, shook every hand. In dance, getting known means getting roles."

It's beginning to pay off. She's starting to get more work, dancing more often. But she still has to depend on welfare, sometimes for months between engagements. Welfare workers don't see dancing as a serious career, or auditions as a proper job search.

"It's pretty easy to get depressed in Montreal, with all the poverty here. For me, I feel I'm in it, but not quite. I mean, I know right now I'm poor, but I believe it's temporary. Since completing my formal training, it seems like nothing but hardship, but out of it I've grown so much more confident, not to mention politically aware. When I'm sitting waiting in the welfare office, I look around, and everyone's so miserable and tense. Sometimes people just lose it and rage, then the cops come and it gets really ugly. I want to go·to the single mother with her three kids and hug her, tell her she's got a right to be upset. It shouldn't be like this, people shouldn't be hungry and homeless in the best country in the world. We have these egomaniacal government dinosaurs with nothing new in their minds. I'm starting to think we don't really live in a democracy—we get to chose between Satan and his brother and that's no choice at all."

Clifford and Alexandra are two young people also trying to make it. She studies social work at McGill University, and he is on welfare.

I met Alexandra, an attractive, intelligent, thoughtful young woman, when she was enlisted as a French-language interpreter for an interview I was trying to conduct at a legal rights organization. If she's learned anything here, it's that: "I never, never, never want to be on welfare."

She cast her lot early: "When I was fifteen, I worked at a designer clothing store. I wouldn't ever say that things looked good on someone when they didn't. I decided I won't be a big person taking from little people: that's what business seems to be doing to people today."

Now, to support herself through school, she works at a designer coffee store. She stays on while others quit in disgust.

"I'm learning a lot about life. These bosses know how badly you need the money. So they have a free hand when it comes to treating you badly: yelling and being as unpleasant as possible with the little power they have."

When she told him what she's been putting up with, her boyfriend, Clifford, told her that she should have quit on the first day.

"Maybe I should have."

Clifford admires her, especially her single-minded pursuit of her goal. He hasn't been able to find steady work, and being on welfare is demoralizing, even though, as he tells me, he's seen much worse in his young life, especially in his early days in Haiti.

"Here at least there are people to help you. The poverty in

Haiti, you can't compare it. You see someone living on the street in Montreal, and you go, oh that poor person, but in Haiti, most people are on the streets, and there is no one to intervene."

His mother lived in New York, and had a good job cleaning office buildings. He stayed with his aunt in Haiti, who was a nurse married to a doctor. They ran a clinic out of their home. There were always a lot of children around.

"A lot of parents couldn't afford to raise their kids, so they'd send them to my aunt's. They weren't treated like maids or anything, but they'd help out with cleaning, cooking. I grew up not having to do anything for myself."

He attended elementary school in Haiti, and it was strict.

"The teachers were allowed to whip you if you did anything bad. Then the parents would have a go when you got home."

He was sent to Montreal to live with yet another aunt. He went to school in Montreal North, starting in grade five.

"I didn't like the teachers. Then another kid in my class stole something and they blamed it on me. I got suspended."

To his aunt, this was a very big thing. She put him on a bus and sent him to his mother in New York.

"I couldn't speak English, just French and Creole, so I was put back to grade three in order to learn the language. I would have been totally lost if it weren't for a couple of Haitian kids I found."

And he loved his other new discovery: television. In about six months, he'd learned enough of the English language from his favourite programs to jump ahead to grade six.

His mother cleaned offices and mopped floors—heavy, hard work—while his stepfather stayed home and criticized him. He was relieved to return with his mother to Montreal, leaving behind his stepfather, and it was in high school that he met Alexandra.

They didn't encounter much trouble as an interracial couple, although some of the black female students weren't too happy with his choice. They both shrugged that off.

Clifford took computer training at a privately run, for-profit school his uncle recommended. It was hard, he confesses, very condensed. He could have used more time to thoroughly understand what he was expected to learn. He gets short-term jobs now—two, three months at a time—but then he's back on social assistance.

"We want to live here, it's our city. We may not have a house with a white picket fence, but we're a stable couple, and we want to make it."

Alexandra has known that she wanted to work with people since she was five years old. "At first, I thought I'd become a cop. I had this distorted view that they actually help people." She sighs for innocence lost.

She wonders sometimes what keeps her going to school, knowing that only service jobs will be waiting when she graduates. "Everything is being cut, everything. It seems the jobs of the future are the jobs at the bottom."

Her father, who left the family home when she was five, encourages her to stick it out: "He tells me to visualize my goal everyday, and I'll achieve it."

She considers herself relatively fortunate in that, by the time she completes her B.A., her student debt will be only $10,000.

Alexandra told me about Laurent Prud'homme, a fifty-three-year-old Montrealer to whom fate and the mindless search for profits dealt a considerable blow. He's a thoughtful, kind, newly politicized individual who cares enough to step outside his own experience and reach out to others. Laurent describes himself as "kind of a square guy." His hair used to be dark blond, now it's greying.

"I'm pretty ordinary looking, always clean-shaven and dressed conservatively. I don't like heavy metal music, I still enjoy the Big Band sound, soft and classical music."

He's been thinking a lot about society and where it's heading.

"Three years ago, I was vice-president and director of a branch of a publishing company, pulling down $75,000 a year. We started it, my friend and I. He was the marketing manager. We got financial backing from three guys in Toronto. I'd spent about eighteen years in the city, working in advertising, first as a translator, then as a junior copywriter, then as an account executive."

He and his friend started an annual publication, listing all the manufacturers of computers and computer parts and software in the market. It was the right idea at the right time, and they soon expanded their endeavours to the extent that revenues were at the $4.5-million mark.

They were in prolonged negotiations with their financial backers about company profit-sharing and stocks when they were called in, asked to hand over the keys to their office and their company cars: the company had been sold to an American firm. And that was it.

"Maybe we should have suspected, but we were naïve. My partner got really depressed. At our age, late forties, jobs in Montreal are hard to come by, even those at a lower level than we were used to. I sold my house in Dorval and my wife's car, bought an old Chevette. A big dip in your standard of living. I figured, better to make even $200 a week than to use up our savings."

He got minimum-wage jobs: telemarketing, polling. It was pretty awful, demoralizing. They would time him on bathroom breaks, listen in to his calls.

"But I was pretty lucky. I already had a sense that I was not my job. Not what I owned or what I made. That's what made the difference between me and my partner."

For eight years Laurent had used his spare time to work as a volunteer for a non-profit group, giving personal development courses to adults in the community from all walks of life. This effort to help others eventually helped him to handle the stress of losing what he'd worked so hard for.

"My partner had been a real health freak, he exercised

regularly, took natural food supplements. Took good care of himself. His depression stopped all that—within a year he'd lost his house. His wife took his daughter and left, telling him he was not the same man she'd married eighteen years ago. And then he died, just a year after they sold the company out from under us. Cancer. He was a professional, a good, good man—to die so tragically. And just because of a crazy lust for more and more money."

Laurent was raised in a middle-class family. His dad worked at General Motors, and his mother, though she stayed home, was very ambitious. They would buy a house, live in it while renovating it, then sell and start again.

"I was painting walls and repairing holes when I was eight years old," he remembers.

"I had friends telling me, and they were right, that I was losing my language living in Toronto." It was suggested to him that he find a nice French girl, and he did. He met his wife in Toronto, where she was part of an exchange program involving civil servants from Quebec and Ontario.

His wife is no longer able to work; arthritis cripples her hands. And she is now sometimes alarmed at how "radical" her husband is becoming.

"I see so many miserable, penniless people who have no idea of the possibilities out there," Laurent tells me. "Maybe it's time that people with wider vision tried to help them."

Laurent believes all the current political parties constitute an *ancien régime*, a blend of old, self-serving ideas and irrelevancies. He talks with his friends about starting a new political party, a party of relevance that would concentrate on job creation, not separation.

PHILIP AMSEL IS MAKING it. He calls himself an aristocrat of welfare, the Cadillac even.

We arrange to meet at the Network Café, opposite the Snowdon Metro station. He's been recommended to me by a McGill social work professor, Eric Shragge, who, along with the Ashers, has provided me with an extensive list of contacts.

Philip's already at a smoking table when I arrive, a pleasant-looking man nursing a coffee, just a bit rumpled. I'm interrupting his two-week vacation, but he doesn't seem to mind at all.

He's on a lot of medication, I can see it in his eyes and in the evident dryness of his lips and mouth. He was diagnosed with paranoid schizophrenia in the 1970s, but has since been rediagnosed as manic depressive. (It often happens that the first label undergoes re-examination and "correction" as the diagnostic flavour of the month changes.)

He takes: Nozanan, 100 milligrams in the evening; three pills of lithium a day; and tops it off with Serax as required. He's been hospitalized four times.

He grew up in a normal middle-class home in Ville St. Laurent, and his childhood was happy enough, he remembers.

He liked to write, had good friends. Life was filled with possibilities.

"Sometimes I think it would have been nice to have kids and a marriage, but I had a very action-filled youth, with lots of partying."

If he regrets anything, and he tries not to, it's his experimentation with "pollutants."

As soon as I hear that word, I have a crystal-clear mental picture of a transparent plastic bag filled to overflowing with oddly shaped pink pills: little amphetamine wonders that made people feel like Superman. Friends of mine, in Dawson College, had a pharmaceutical connection that made them as available as candy, and we swallowed them as if they were.

You never got hungry, you could stay up round the clock, you could outrace the fastest car—or at least you felt you could. The downs were unpleasant, leaving you strung-out and paranoid, so the trick was to stay up, postpone the crash as long as possible, or mellow it out with pot or beer.

I remember feeling the pills were making me a little too crazy, and going off them cold turkey after months. I was walking down a school corridor when I started sweating buckets. It drenched my clothes, and I had to hide in the bathroom till that, and the shaking, stopped.

Philip thought they gave him an edge, made him smarter, cleverer. What they actually made him was psychotic, resulting in his original misdiagnosis, and of course treatment with medications inappropriate to the "disease."

"When people I'd gone to school with were building their careers, I was in a mental hospital."

He struggled his way back into the normal work world—he has a business background in real estate. He smiles at me, wondering if I can visualize him in his former office on de Maisonneuve, wearing, he assures me, a suit.

He's been an activist for it seems like forever. He used to be president of the Notre-Dame-de-Grâce (NDG) anti-poverty group I visited earlier, but now he's involved in an Urban Issues Program, funded by a grant from the Bronfmans. If you work for a community program while on welfare, you can get about $800 a month.

He divides his time between the NDG community council food bank, putting out a newsletter in which he sometimes writes editorials, and community theatre. In the last play he was involved in, he played the welfare agent.

"It's okay for rich people to go to movies and plays just to be entertained, but the poor have to go to an 'education,'" he muses. Still, it's a good learning tool. "We always have a hero or heroine with a problem, like a single mom trying to go back to school. We stop the action, say the landlord or the welfare worker is yelling at her, 'You just don't want to work,'"—and, he adds thoughtfully, some people are like that, but it may be because they're afraid of failing again—"we'll stop the action and ask the audience—most of whom have been in similar circumstances—what she should say or do."

He's lucky to have been able to rent from an elderly couple in Snowdon, who appreciate their quiet tenant enough to charge him only $400. Philip thought it wise to leave NDG, where he could never get away from his work. He was constantly running into people in need, or who wanted to discuss this and that. You have to develop survival mechanisms if you want to last as an activist.

There is so much to do, and so few resources, personal and otherwise, to call on to get things done. He's closer to the ground than Annette, without a trace of ideology, and perhaps he finds it easier to communicate with his peers than she does.

As our conversation winds down, a man comes in with his child and stops, after an instant of surprised recognition, to chat with Philip. They used to sell real estate out of the same office, and it's an awkward conversation, both participants pretty self-conscious.

I can't help but wonder how many similar encounters between the mainstream employed and their "disappeared" former colleagues occur every day in the city.

CHAPTER SIX

ST. JOHN'S

Prescott Inn

I LANDED EARLY—VERY, very early—on a Sunday morning. The plane was an hour late taking off from Toronto. And to make matters worse, the video wouldn't work for either of the two in-flight movies they tried to show us. The pilot kept thanking us—rather hopefully, I thought—for our understanding.

I was feeling a bit disoriented, because it took me a while to figure out that St. John's is actually an hour and a half ahead of Toronto—not just the usual "half hour later in Newfoundland." So Sunday was pretty much a write-off.

This bed-and-breakfast is a no-smoking establishment; guests are asked to confine their smoking to the balconies. At close to 2:00 a.m. I can't find one, so I creep down three floors and sit on the outside stoop. It's quiet, as you would expect at that time—a relief from the airport, which was crowded and hectic and almost festive.

I hear footsteps coming up the street, and a guttural, choking, wordless cry filled with rage. A hugely angry young man, hair cut short enough to qualify him as a skinhead, carrying his shirt in one clenched fist, storms past me, radiating the kind of fury that in an American city would result in gunfire. When my heart kicks in again, I pray that he's not going home to a wife, to children. I'm happy to lock the door behind me and return to my room, and bed.

I've come to St. John's, the last city on my tour, armed with information, names and phone numbers. Ever since my first trip through the Maritimes (getting as far as Prince Edward Island twice), I've heard that Newfoundland has a different kind of beauty. In my head, this translated to a lot of little villages and bare rock thrusting out of the Atlantic. I wasn't prepared for parks, and green hills, and men and women wearing business clothes, instead of the stereotypical yellow rubber fishermen's gear and knee-high rubber Billy boots.

The rows of houses come in all different colours—pink and blue and purple and every shade under the St. John's sun— and every third building or so, it seems, bears a historical plaque. It's stunningly beautiful, like entering a Grimm's Fairy Tale world where houses are made of spun sugar and candy. The people are strange and enticing, hard-faced and worry-worn, until you smile, and then they are transformed into proud and welcoming Newfoundlanders.

I used to love Vancouver, with the rugged mountains looming over the city; I used to feel a deep pride in being a Montrealer; but St. John's makes you ache in your very bones. I want to stay here.

I've been looking forward to this visit more than any other, carrying with me high expectations of a different kind of poverty, one without the stigma that generally afflicts the poor. If everyone is struggling, surely that must foster tolerance and understanding, I hope. I almost don't want to delve below the surface, don't want to break the illusion. That tension stays the whole time I'm here.

But every fairy tale has its horrors.

ACROSS THE STREET FROM the Prescott Inn, in Bannerman Park, a "Peace-A-Chord" festival is being held. I find it odd that the first banner, a sheet painted with bold letters, reads:

FREE BURMA

REMEMBER THE FALLEN CHILDREN, MONKS, STUDENTS

8/8/88

3,000 DEAD

Bannerman Park gives me a first glimpse of the city, and some of the concerns and preoccupations of its young activists. And God, are they young.

At most, a hundred people are seated on mats or blankets or towels, singles and couples and groups, in front of a stage where a band called Shaman is performing. In the audience, there are three or four punks, hair up in spikes, with leather collars and pierced body parts; two very self-conscious "Goth" girls in trailing black cloaks; some kids in tie-dyed T-shirts and long hair playing Frisbee; a few middle-aged, ordinarily dressed supporters; and then the majority, regular-looking kids out for a nice time. There is a lot of smoking—cigarettes are passed along and shared like joints.

There's an open tent with a scattering of tables holding leaflets and newsletters and media statements near the band-stand. Oxfam is there, a place to buy "ethical" coffee, and a brave, lonely guy sitting at a gay information table. I compli-ment him on his T-shirt, with its twist on a deodorant slogan: Strong enough for a woman, but made for a man. I also sug-gest that I suspect this is a hard place to be gay.

He tells me that the gay community here—such as it is—has been trying to establish a strong voice, pretty much unsuc-cessfully, for a good twenty years. But he's hopeful.

I tease him a bit. "Well, it's obvious you've made some headway, at least according to the graffiti I saw downtown. It didn't say 'Leo is Queer,' like you might expect in an adolescent insult, it said 'Leo is Gay.'"

He laughs, lets me know there is an Amazon Lesbian organization in St. John's, and I walk away with a few more newsletters.

I ENJOY A WONDERFUL breakfast at the Inn (100 percent better than Montreal's offering), and then, following the advice of the helpful owner and staff, I make my way downtown.

Anytime I've asked anyone remotely connected with tourism, I've been told that there is no homelessness here, no public begging. Strolling down Water Street, St. John's main drag running just above the harbour, I'm at first inclined to believe it. Street corners throughout the truncated shopping district—prime panhandling locations—go unoccupied. I see no messy heaps of sleeping bags and newspapers, no public living. It's not until I reach Atlantic Place, opposite the Supreme Court building, with its food court and businesses, that I'm politely asked for spare change. I almost shout Eureka!

Odd, the things you miss when you're far from home ...

Chris, my panhandler, is sitting on the steps. Relatively young, clean-looking, blond hair tied back, he's outfitted totally in varying shades of black, from his topcoat to his shoes. I counter his request for money with an offer to buy him lunch at the restaurant of his choice if he'll chat with me. His initial suspicion disappears when I explain to him that I want to interview him for a book. We go to the food court inside the building and order from the Burger King. Most of the people sitting around here are connected to the Supreme Court building across the street. Chris points to a table near us and says, "That's the police table. Over there the prison guards sit together.

"Everyone knows everyone here, that's why I hit you up," he explains. "You didn't look familiar, so you must be a tourist."

Chris was born in Germany, raised in British Columbia. When he was fourteen, his parents were killed in a car crash. "B.C. has the highest rate of car crashes in Canada," he informs me solemnly.

He struck out on his own. His father had been a kind of survivalist, encouraging his son's independence and sharing odd skills with him. Like creating bombs out of aerosol cans. Like living off the land.

"He worked for the air force. And my mom, well, she was just my mom."

He's twenty-two and he's been in St. John's for a year and a half, interrupted by a short, frozen sojourn in Montreal in the winter of 1997, just in time for the ice storm that paralyzed that city and left him stranded at a truck stop, eating steak for a week.

"Never thought I'd get sick of steak," he grins.

I tell him he's bucking a trend, coming out here from B.C. when everyone else is going the other way.

"That's why I'm here. I kept hearing about the place from people I met, and I decided to check it out myself. You know, here, there's two hundred good people for every asshole you run into, not like Toronto or Montreal, where there's two hundred assholes for every good guy. Here, someone will come up to you and say, 'Hey boy, you're looking bone thin,' and they'll buy you a chocolate bar.

"I was on television here a couple of times, you know, like, this is a homeless person. There's only a couple of us in St. John's: three, four at the most. People recognized my face, knew I didn't have a place to live. For a while there, panhandling was pretty good. Probably got four, five hundred bucks 'cause of it. Excuse me a minute?"

He's spotted a pack of Players someone's left behind on a table near the window. He comes back grinning—it's almost a full pack.

"I like Mondays, everyone's forgetful."

He never graduated from grade school. Whatever education he has, he picked up on his travels.

"Vancouver's not the greatest place on the planet. It's all right, but one deadly place if you don't know what you're doing. That's one of the reasons I came here, to a place where people don't try and kill you."

He's been in some serious trouble here and there. In Toronto, he and two friends, all of them highly stoned, decided to take down an arcade on Yonge Street. They were armed, and they were caught. He did some rough time.

"I remember my first time in Toronto, I bedded down—I had a little pup tent—in Regent Park, and during the night there was a battle between two gangs, and there I was right in the middle of it."

Two bullets hit him; one lodged close to his spine. He spent six months in hospital. He's also had his wrist broken, courtesy of a crowbar-wielding truck driver.

"In Toronto I had to act like a giant tough guy. When I was in Montreal, I acted deaf and dumb, so nobody'd beat me up for not speaking French."

He's learned how not to aggravate the police, how to avoid confrontations.

"Never look at them. If it's illegal to panhandle, you just leave a hat on the ground and stay still. Never make eye contact. I know everywhere they're trying to stop us panhandling. Welfare's at an all-time low. It's like they're trying to exterminate us slowly. But there's no way government's going to win. There's more and more homeless all the time, and we got to eat, got to live. Oh, shit," he says, looking over at the table where he snagged the smokes, "they must be hers."

He's up and over to a table where a tired woman is digging through her purse. He speaks softly to her, but she's shaking her head and he's back, smiling again.

"Not hers. She's very nice. Gives me coffee a lot of times."

It's lucky I caught him today, because this will be his last day in St. John's. He points out the window at the hills with their baby trees. "I'm hungry for real trees. That's only as high as they grow here. Tonight I'll hitch a ride to Gander, then to Port-aux-Basques, catch a boat to North Sydney. I'll meet my friend there, he's driving a truck to B.C. I know people everywhere in this country."

A woman comes to our table. Leaning over and speaking quietly, she asks Chris for the cigarettes. They belong to someone who works upstairs, she explains, and he'll be back to look for them. He shrugs, and hands them over.

"What's going to happen when you get tired of the life?" I ask him.

"I figure by the time I'm forty-five, social services will have to get off its ass and give me money to live on. I've never been greedy, I lived like my father taught me. I don't believe like he did that the world's going to blow up, but I can take care of myself. And I'm set in my ways. I've got no bills, no rules—hell, I'm afraid I'd be a real slob if I lived in a place. I've never had to clean up after myself."

"You never found a worker you could connect to? Someone who could help you with things like housing and welfare?"

"Oh sure, you meet some nice people. But they always leave, they get to know you and they're gone. And some of them, well, you tell them about yourself and they start to cry." He shakes his head in disgust. "That's not helping. The thing I like about the people here in St. John's, you can fuck up majorly and people will still like you."

He asks a woman at the next table for the time. While she looks at her watch, a man sitting with her says, with edgy anger, "You don't know the time." She ignores him and says, "It's one-thirty." Chris thanks her politely.

"What do you believe in, Chris?" I ask, as we smoke a last cigarette.

"You can't afford beliefs, living on the street. They get crushed too much."

As we're heading out, we stop to talk to a lady that works in a store in the building. He tells her he wants to say good-bye, that he's heading out to B.C.

"Well, you take care of yourself, Chris."

"I will."

We walk past the security desk, and he points to it and says, "See? Nobody's even on duty till one guy comes about four o'clock. It really is different here."

Outside, we hug goodbye, and I watch him walk away. His leaving will cut St. John's homeless population by a third. In Vancouver, he'll be just another drop in an ocean of the dispossessed.

He told me that he'd like to live forever, "See what happens to the world. Does it make it?"

Does he?

OUTSIDE ATLANTIC PLACE, a little to the left, away from the stairs, stands Don, an older man in odd clothes. Cut-off jeans are one thing, but cut-off (just above the shins) plaid polyester pants make quite another fashion statement.

I stop to chat, and he answers my question about how lucrative he's finding the day with a laugh. "Oh, my love, it's not bad, not bad." He explains why he's panhandling by pointing, strangely, down to his shoes. "I have a hernia, you see. I'm supposed to have an operation but I don't want to, doctors scare me." But when I out myself as a crazy who wants to have a look at the Waterford Hospital, Newfoundland's sprawling red-brick mental institution, he comes clean.

"No, my dear, you don't want to go there. That's a sick hospital. Sick." Every two weeks, he goes there for his shot, but he never stays long. It seems that Don represents the schizophrenic problem in St. John's.

He's been to Toronto, he says, where he picked up a drinking problem and got depressed from "living out in the weather."

He used kill seals for a living, he tells me, watching closely for any evidence of censure. But that's all gone now, like everything else. Even the winters aren't the same, don't get bad ones like you did years ago. "Yes, my dear, I remember when there was all kinds of snow, and the codfish, you know."

People treat him pretty well, he says; mostly he panhandles to pay for his "bad habit," cigarettes, and for extra bits of food.

He shares a place with a woman who's had a hard life; she "lost her husband a few years back" when he choked on his own vomit in a bar.

"Are you religious at all?" he asks me, after I pass him a couple of two-dollar coins.

"Yes," I reassure him, "I'm a Muslim."

His brow furrows just a bit. "And what's that, then?"

"Same God," I shorthand, not wanting to get into a discussion of comparative religion.

He's pleased, and he gives me his blessing, which I undoubtedly need.

OPPOSITE MY B & B, back at Bannerman Park where no one sleeps at night, I encounter a kid gang. I've been assuming that there are two in town, but I'm beginning to suspect that it's actually the same one moving between this park and the war memorial on Duckworth, above Water Street.

They don't wear colours or leather jackets, but they all have skateboards, and they're all practising moves. Irreverently, the boys rumble down the stairs of the nearby government building, cheered on by their girlfriends, and surprisingly they are not chased away by irate security guards. It is clear from their ages that this problem will resolve itself when they all go back to school.

Up the street is a well-organized, brightly lit and well-stocked variety store. On my way in I'm hit up by a panhandler with a nose for a bargain. His name is Bill. He's a senior, and a well-known character.

Usually, he explains to me, one Coke will cost you almost a dollar, but they're having a sale: two for $1.01. He can't let that go by, so I augment his change and follow him inside, where he is greeted by name and treated like a valued customer. He walks me back to my room, clutching his plastic bag with two soft drinks, bemoaning the fact that his new shoes "with the toes still in them" have turned out to be too small for his feet.

His brother will be coming soon, and will clear up his debts, which he assures me are major. That same brother has offered to open a bank account for him, deposit a lot of money, but he's refused, telling him that five minutes after it was done, he'd have welfare after him for a meeting, "And they'd grab every last cent of it."

Matthew DellaValle is giving himself, and the system, another chance. I meet him up the street from the Prescott Inn at Emmanuel House Community Centre and Residence, a government-funded housing program. The Centre offers a four-month program, with both individual and group counselling as well as life-skills training, that deals with problems such as the effects of depression, abuse, addiction and joblessness.

Matthew is a tall, good-looking man, twenty-eight years old. He was born in Newfoundland, in a small fishing village hit hard by the tidal wave in 1929, which destroyed houses and took lives. A psychic has predicted that another wave will happen this week, and some folks are a bit edgy, keeping an eye on the ocean.

We're out on the back deck, sitting at a picnic table. It's the house's "smoking room."

Matthew and his sister were born "out of wedlock" to a mother who was a drinker. He remembers, when he was six, his mother taking them to his father's lover's sister's house, dropping them off and promising she'd be back at four o'clock. She never came back.

The children were fostered out, sent to the mainland and put up for adoption. They lived for a year with a family in Grimsby, Ontario. At the end of that year, he was told that the family could not keep both of them, and that they had decided to adopt his sister. He was fostered out again, to families in the same community, and finally a family on the same street as his sister's took him in.

"We were divided by a highway. We'd yell at each other across the road, that kind of thing."

His was a good family. The couple had two children, but they "never treated me any less than their own." The foster father taught math at the local high school. The mom was a nurse, but she stayed home to look after Matthew, because "there was so much shit going on" inside of him. "They got me at a real bad time. I was a torn-up, beat-up kid." He didn't understand why he did things that caused trouble. He was running away regularly, partly because he hated school, where he was teased and tormented.

The couple was planning to adopt him, but the arrangement was terminated instead and he was made a ward of the Crown, and thereby condemned to a future of shifting foster home placements—fourteen in all—and the occasional group home.

"Even my birthdate's been changed four or five times. I didn't know who I was. Or even if I was normal. I'd look at myself and I'm wondering if I'm thinking right. I couldn't say, 'Hey Dad, is thinking like this normal?' I didn't know what emotions to have. It got so overwhelming at times."

He was shifted from Grimsby to Welland, from Welland to Niagara-on-the-Lake, from there to Port Colborne, then back to Welland, where he was put into an independent-living program at sixteen years of age, unsupervised but with some financial support. There was no pressure to go to school. His rent was paid for him, and he got twenty-five dollars a week to eat. But he got in trouble there, too.

"I had a roommate who was a bit of a criminal. The television in our place was hot. So I got a Young Offenders record." He was put on a year's probation and sent to yet another foster home, this one in Niagara Falls.

Meanwhile, his sister had been bugging her adoptive parents to look for her real mother. Her relationship with her adoptive family was strained, and eventually fell apart, but not before they discovered that their mother lived within 100 kilometres of them. She was on welfare. Matthew went to live with her. He found he had two half-brothers, one in his thirties, the other in his late twenties. Both were still at home, and unemployed.

"But they were always looking for work."

Money was very tight. They lived in a big old run-down house, and most of their mom's welfare cheque went for rent.

"My mom was a little religious, into fundamentalist Christian stuff. Her oldest boy was wound up all the time. He'd get a bit aggressive if he didn't get his way. I liked the other brother, he was laid back, smoked dope and read books all the time we picked out of bins. He was a smart fellow. A true hippie, radical in mind and spirit."

They lived by scavenging. "We'd tie four or five shopping carts together and walk down the streets, looking from side to side, just like we were shopping in a real store. People would stare at us, and we'd say, you know, 'Hey, do you mind? We're just buying our groceries here.' We'd recycle everything."

Six months with his mother was all he could handle. If he did anything wrong, she'd say: "'Get thee hence, Satan,' and crap like that. After a while, I said, 'That's it! I'm out of here.'"

He was eighteen when he found himself on the streets in Toronto. It was exciting, a twenty-four-hour lifestyle. He'd hang out in front of Sam the Record Man's, panhandling for the price of a room. "My home was Yonge Street. At night, I'd sleep on top of restaurants. I'd climb up on dumpsters, throw my pack up, and then throw the rest of me up."

He tried to stay away from the temptations of drugs, because, "You can't be fucked up out here." He'd do some pot, and occasionally some coke—mostly to stay awake, because you could freeze to death in the night. He'd run across dead bodies in alleyways.

The shelters were a little crazy. "The winos could get real obnoxious. There'd be fights and yelling." It felt cleaner being outside. "I met a lot of punkers, and buskers. They're sensible people, the buskers. You look at them and think they're only concentrating on their music, but they always know what's happening on the street. They're the eyes and ears of the community. Better than a newspaper."

He got in tight with a group called SkinHeads Against Racial Prejudice (SHARP).

"We were always fighting with neo-Nazis. I got a reputation as a hard guy. My street name was Bulldog. We had blacks, Chinese, Vietnamese in our group. We'd informally patrol the streets and alleyways, looking out for skinheads bothering people. The neo-Nazis would try to chase the poor off their corners. I watched both groups for a while, and I saw that, instead of a boot in the face, or stealing whatever money a person had managed to panhandle, the guys from SHARP were gentle. I mean, it was touching, the difference. They became like a role model to me. That really nice Italian family that had tried to adopt me, they taught me to hate Nazism. They left Italy in the first place 'cause of Mussolini. Hitler was such a monster, and he's still leaving an impact on kids today. Being a deep thinker, I've thought a lot about that."

He came back to Newfoundland a year ago.

"I wasn't getting anywhere. Still the same, no money, no foundation, nothing to show for everything I'd gone through. No education, struggling every day just to eat. Couldn't get work, most places want at least grade twelve. And I burnt out on restaurant work. You think it would be different here, but people look at you like 'You suck cause you're poor.' I get my chops busted all the time, people say, 'How come you're on welfare?' Christ, I was raised up dependent on the government for everything. My life was directly controlled by the system. At first, you know, for a short period of time, being a ward of the Crown made me feel important. The government were my parents. But now I'm grown up."

This is his second tour of Emmanuel House. He blew it the first time, when he got hooked on the government-operated VLTs in the downtown bars.

"I was spending my rent money, my food money. Sometimes I'd win, and I'd feel so good, I'd be able to pay off my debts, buy nice things, all the basics. Mostly I'd lose. I'm ninety days clean."

He wants to get into activism. "I see myself one day being mayor of this town, and maybe even beyond that. I wouldn't care who I pissed off. I'd say 'This is reality, and this isn't.' I'd get to the root of the problems out there."

He was profiled on the local cable channel's "Community Matters" program. He talked about homelessness, and the underhoused. The private landlords who own lots of row houses, with no smoke-detectors, no fire escapes, rats. "They violate every rule in the book and get way with it 'cause people are afraid to complain."

Matthew's going to be a daddy soon: a one-night stand who swore (he says) she couldn't get pregnant. She's keeping the baby, but "being real mean" about letting him into the picture.

"I want to be there for my kid. I don't want her questioning whether or not she's normal. I'm going to be a reasonable dad, going to let her make her own decisions."

I ask him about his awareness of the dangers of unprotected sex.

"I'm a lucky person when it comes to that." So far.

Right now, he reads a lot. He's taking educational upgrading and wants to study political science and sociology. He's optimistic, and well liked here. Whether or not that's enough, only time will tell.

I MET DOUG ON one of my first days in St. John's, before I'd really figured out the geography of the place. Wandering around, getting lost, I flagged a cab:

"Can you take me downtown?" I asked the driver, a curly-haired man, neatly dressed, and a smoker like me.

He turned and grinned. "This is it, my dear. You're on the main drag, Water Street, but I'll show you around, if you want." And so he did, giving thumbnail reviews of bars and restaurants.

Towards the end of our truncated tour, he asked why I was in St. John's. When I told him, he shook his head slowly. "I know about all that," he said, referring to the topic of poverty. "You heard about Mount Cashel? See 'The Boys of St. Vincent'? I was in there, sent by my mother."

The Mount Cashel Orphanage, run by the Catholic Church, was the site of countless cases of sexual abuse perpetrated by the teachers, an order of Christian Brothers, over the decades. The crimes came to light in 1989, the facility was closed for good in 1990, and many of the Brothers were eventually brought to justice. The story was later shown on television, somewhat fictionalized, as "The Boys of St. Vincent."

Doug swung around to a red brick building called the T. I. Murphy Centre.

"This is named after one of the Christian Brothers. He didn't abuse anyone that I know of. He was a strict man, a disciplinarian, but fair. You ever see the Alfred Hitchcock program on television, you know that profile of him just before the show starts? That's what he looked like, just like that."

We agreed to meet on his day off, Wednesday, for supper. That turned out to be a no go; his car's engine burned out and he had to meet his brother and go to see a mechanic, so we got together Thursday night instead.

Originally we had decided to eat at The Cellar, but, having arrived early, I go inside, and it seems way too upscale and hushed to serve our purposes; you need a little noise around for privacy. Besides, there are no smoking tables available, though I'm informed that we could step into the cigar area, a collection of expensive couches in a closed-off room. When we meet up, we decide instead on an English pub. We are seated at a booth, but not before we've walked past three VLTs.

He orders a hard drink in a tall glass. I stick with Diet Coke.

"I was born in Cuckold's Cove, in 1945, and lived for a time in a house there that was more of a shack. No proper walls, just the bare studs of the outside frame sticking out. No indoor plumbing or electricity. It blew down while I was away, so they told me when I went back to look for it.

"When I was born, my mom already had eight kids. Reg and Eugene and I were at home, Patsy and Louise were in a girls' orphanage. Lorraine died real young. I had an older brother living in Montreal, he had a job and a wife there. Mom took us there in '53, stayed for one school year, came back in '54. Mom rented a narrow three-storey house on John Street, right near where I picked you up on Sunday, behind the Delta? That whole side was torn down, some years ago.

"I remember, in November of '54, two days before my ninth birthday, her saying she had to take us somewhere, she couldn't keep us any more, me and my two younger brothers. The man she was married to wasn't our father, only the oldest kids' dad. I didn't know where she was taking us, but I remember crying, begging her to wait just the two days till my birthday, but she wouldn't.

"Her and Uncle Sam—he wasn't our uncle but we called him that—took us up by bus, and I couldn't stop bawling. I remember Sam saying to me, 'Stop crying, or they're gonna call you a sissy.' I didn't give a damn if anyone saw me crying, what bothered me was that they were going to leave me there. The hardest thing of all was her not waiting for my birthday. Nothing else was as painful as that. I didn't even think about the two youngest, I felt totally isolated, totally alone. She never, ever showed again, didn't hear nothing for six years. I remember two incidents that day, the youngest boy peeing on the Brother's couch, and me crying."

He doesn't remember much of his early life with his mom, doesn't remember a lot of hitting or a lot of hugging. She was a heavy drinker, and was said to have played around a lot. There were three different fathers for the eight children.

He does recall the physical and sexual abuse at Mount

Cashel. As he talks, it becomes very clear that he is deeply conflicted about what happened to him there, and that he carries a lot of guilt for not looking out for his brothers.

He was in the band, learning trumpet, "and this Brother started saying, 'You could be really good.' Then he started coming to my bunk. For the first six months, he was gentle, kind and soft. Other than the initial fright, he never threatened me, never used force. Looking back, there were times when it could be nice."

But he suspected that wouldn't be the end of it. When the Brother would come to his bunk, he'd roll over on his stomach to avoid being fondled. They never anally penetrated him.

"I often wondered, later on, if they had some kind of secret code, or a system—like, if one of them was molesting you, everyone else would leave you alone. Nobody talked about what was happening. I can't recall ever, no one, not even myself, saying anything about it. The main thing was fear, that's how we related to each other, including me against you. The more I intimidated you, the more likely I could get your butter or your dessert tonight at supper. Wasn't till the last two years, I stopped tippytoeing, started saying no, started saying 'I'm gonna tell.'

"I became a real tyrant in the place, and I started running away. It was weird, I was always found in Cuckold's Cove. Even though my mother wasn't there, that's where I went. Got punished, of course. They'd convince you that you been so bad you deserved whatever you got from them.

"The very worst, worse even than being molested—'cause that was dark, and private, and you could pretend no one knew—the very worst was being beaten by four of the Brothers. There I was lying naked on my back, screaming, knowing that they could hear me out there, the others, that they knew what was happening to me."

In spite of everything, he did well at the school. He regularly came first or second in his class. He wonders, if he had stayed, if there hadn't been abuse, what he might have been able to accomplish in his life.

He was called over to the Brothers' side of the building one day. "He asked me, one of them, 'Would you like to go to Montreal?' I said yes right away. 'The plane leaves in three hours.'"

Six years had gone by. It was July 1960.

"My two youngest brothers never got out till weeks later. I felt so happy to be leaving that I never saw, though I see it now, the hurt in their eyes. I found out, I saw the telegram, that the Brothers had told my mother if she didn't take me back they'd have to send me to reform school, 'cause of my behaviour. That's why she sent for me.

"She met me at the airport with two men, Ronnie and Stu were their names. She was waitressing, and she lived in a one-room apartment with a private bathroom and a shared kitchen. It was one or two streets shy of Guy, downtown. I never knew till they were busted that her two friends were bank robbers. Remember that plague of robberies that went on in Montreal back then? They were younger than mum, but nice to me. No 'Get out of my way, you little creep.' They treated me almost like an adult. There was an awful lot of drinking and card playing, and they talked pretty plain in front of me. Didn't tone down their language, but they also didn't talk about the job they'd done last week, or the one they'd do next."

He stayed with his mum for a short while, till she lost her job and she couldn't afford the rent. "She couldn't get a pillow slip out of Family Services or the Federation of Catholic Charities. I got placed in Weredale for six months."

"No shit!?" I drop my pen for a moment and we swap stories about the Weredale Boys' Home, a combination orphanage and home for troubled teens. I once worked with kids from there, advocating for them against a very authoritarian administration.

"There were an awful lot of weird goings-on late at night, seemed like even more than Mount Cashel."

His mom got a three-bedroom house in Notre-Dame-de-Grâce, finally, through the Salvation Army, and he was back at home. He hooked up with a friend he'd met in Weredale, and together they started shoplifting, breaking and entering and purse-snatching. They were finally caught breaking into a Verdun pool hall.

While out on personal recognizance awaiting trial for that, he and another friend were downtown at the Blue Angel when an American gentleman kept coming on to them. They led him into an alley, where his friend clipped the guy behind the ear, grabbed his wallet and ran. Doug got two years in Bordeaux Jail.

"Before they'd been pretty lenient, but it seemed like they got fed up with my antics, you know, 'Hey, we gotta start getting a little tougher.' They'd given me a job in the holding area, cleaning showers, collecting towels. The stuff I witnessed there turned me around dramatically. The beatings, the rapes. From 1968 to now, that's thirty years, I've never willfully stolen a nickel."

He met his first wife in Boston. He was working as a supervisor in a paper mill, making good money. He had a home worth about $60,000, with a $30,000 mortgage. He had an old car that was paid for, and a new car he was making payments on, and a real problem catching up to him.

He's not a regular drinker, but a deep one—he could drink fifteen shots in one night, and then not touch liquor again for months. His wife wasn't that lucky: she was heavily into booze and pills and whatever else might be available. They had a daughter; she was six when he left.

"It was 1979. I truthfully, wholeheartedly believed if I didn't leave, my daughter would be an orphan, because I was going to kill her mom." He left his wife the house and the old car, took the new one and its payment schedule, and drove back to Newfoundland. Even though they didn't speak much, she faithfully sent their daughter to St. John's every summer to be with her dad.

One Christmas, after she was grown up and doing a stint in the Armed Forces, the daughter came home on leave to find her mom in a coma: the result of a forty-ouncer a day and tranquillizers, a lethal combination. She died without regaining consciousness.

Doug's daughter is married and getting out of the service this week, and wants her dad to come live with them.

Just recently separated from his second wife and their child, Doug is living in a good-sized room on the second floor of a house; he shares a kitchen and the third-floor bathroom. He pays $325 a month, and just recently got a phone.

"It's the first real time I've been on my own and I do not like it. Now I'm dreading even more because I blew the engine out of my car." It affects his freedom, his ability to get out and see his daughter and his wife. He wants to keep that relationship good, but there is also a practical side: his wife still does his laundry, including ironing the "collar shirts" and pants he needs to keep his taxi-driving job.

It might take him three or four months to save enough to afford another used vehicle. He could get one in the range of six hundred to a thousand dollars, but then there's the registration and insurance, all adding up. Maybe twelve to fifteen hundred to put it on the road. He works six days a week as it is, taking home twelve thousand.

He expects to leave Newfoundland in about eight months, to look for work in the States. His child by his second wife, daughter Megan, will be twelve.

"I've been gearing her up for about two years, about how hard it is to get good work here. And her best friend's father— he worked for Hibernia—lost his job and now he's out in Alberta. So she's pretty aware."

Doug's problems weigh him down, and so does his past. Five years ago, he was contacted by a team investigating the abuses at Mount Cashel as part of a civil suit. "I remember telling the guy, 'You must be crazy! I'm forty-seven, those guys have got to be in their eighties if they're not dead.' But you know, it turns out two of them were only twelve or thirteen years older than me. They were only twenty-one, twenty-two, when I was nine."

It's been a difficult five years.

"Before that, life wasn't great but I was doing okay. I must tell you I have a great attraction for women. I've been married twice, engaged once, and lived for a while with another woman. I have no homosexual urges. But it seems like I just can't sustain my feelings for women over time. After the initial lust dies down, making love seems more like a chore, and lately, well, it's got worse. I even went to a doctor to get myself checked out physically. I'm fifty-two, in good health, good shape. I could understand if it was a war wound or the result of a car crash, but this?"

I ask him what he thinks the problem is, and he says, "Nobody ever taught me what love is supposed to be. I still don't think I know. There's a fine lady at Victims' Services who's trying to connect me with a counsellor."

The investigators have assured him that when the next trials start, they will pay all his expenses to come back and testify. He doesn't expect it to get any easier.

"I watched two of the Brothers come into court. My stomach turned to ice, my palms soaking wet," he tells me, running his hand under his glass of rye and coke, showing me the little pool collected. "They both looked fairly healthy. One was a bit stooped, shrivelled-looking, the other fairly straight, wearing a hat and glasses with chains on them that made him look a bit foppish."

And actually giving testimony?

"I found in the courtroom giving testimony I was able to look at them straight in the eye. I could hear the quivering in my voice, hear my heart beating, but at the same time I wondered what they were feeling. They sat there, motionless, emotionless. I considered that I might not be believed by the judge, but that didn't matter because I knew that they knew I had them in my sights. It didn't matter what anyone else thought. You know, I've sat at the same kind of table where they were sitting, listening to people tell what I did when I was just a J.D. [juvenile delinquent], and knowing they were telling the truth. It's a hard thing. The prosecutors said that even if they didn't have any other witness, my testimony would have been enough. Still, you know what it's like when you feel really sick, and you force yourself to vomit? That's what I felt, more relief than fear or gladness. I'm sorry I'm going through it. Even if I get money out of it, I'll still be sorry. This part of the aftermath, this trouble I'm experiencing . . . I'm not looking forward to continuing. But I know they would benefit if I stopped. I would be the bad guy."

THE NEXT AFTERNOON, I'M sitting in a car with Sarah Sharp and her two-year-old German shepherd, and we're parked across the street from where Mount Cashel once loomed so large in the lives of the children entrusted to it. It's torn down now; the field is ploughed up, ready for a new housing development.

"They should salt the earth," I remark.

Sarah sighs heavily. She too believes that the evil will reassert itself, perhaps taking the form of abuse within the walls of these new structures.

I'd heard about Sarah pretty consistently since landing in St. John's. People are mighty proud of her, and I kept saying to them and to myself, "I think I know this woman."

"Well sure you do," she laughed over the phone. "And I've

often wondered what happened to that fine young woman with all those good ideas."

I must have met Sarah fifteen, twenty years ago, when I had a brief flirtation with the board of the National Anti-Poverty Organization. Brief because I felt, being just slightly over-sensitive in those days, that having a social worker in charge as executive director was not a good idea. But Sarah was very real, down-to-earth and supportive; she made a real difference to the organization. Hearing her voice brought back all the positive feelings she engendered. Now she's on disability, because of the injury she received when she was hit by a postal van—she's won the poverty lottery. She's forty-eight years old, and she already has eight grandchildren.

In her usual no-nonsense, take-charge manner, she refused my offer to come and meet her, saying it would be too long a haul. Instead she picked me up and asked me what I wanted to see. First stop: Signal Hill, where Marconi received by wireless telegraphy the first transatlantic communication. The view was as spectacular as people had told me it would be, the ocean spreading out in front, St. John's huddled in the back—it does something to your heart.

The Mount Cashel site was our next stop, and once we'd seen enough we made our way back to the car. Sarah walks painfully, with a cane. She tells me about her family history, and offers to show me "the red brick building where my dad used to live"—the Waterford.

Sarah's father was from an affluent family of merchants. He'd "done the whole thing" in his youth—everything the children of the wealthy are given—including piano lessons. His brothers and sisters are all business people; his cousins all have university degrees. Her dad was an independent fellow, and lied about his age to join the merchant marine during World War II when he was fifteen. He had the experience of two ships being torpedoed out from under him, and witnessed the loss of life. It was to prey on his mind for years to come.

At home, he established a business in interior/exterior decorating, as well as running a mechanics shop with a friend. For a time, they lived pretty well; their clothes came from the Sears and Eaton's catalogues. Sarah remembers being the richest family in their small neighbourhood: "We were so proud, we weren't allowed to speak to the family next door because they were on welfare." They had the first black-and-white television on the street: "People'd come in and sit in front of the fridge and wait for it to come on."

"Dad never listened to anyone. He was too independent, vocal and outspoken. He told it like it was. When his mother offered him a particular bit of land, one he didn't like, his response was along the lines of 'Shove it up your arse.' They didn't get along much after that."

Her mother "had six children on the floor" when her husband first suffered a breakdown and went to the Waterford mental hospital. A lawyer friend arranged the sale of the businesses and set up a trust fund for the family, but even so their fortunes had changed. Nobody used the word "poor" in those days; if you were having financial problems, you were "stuck," and they were stuck.

"Dad had made good friends with the lawyers and doctors he'd done decorating for. We never went without on Christmas, we'd get food hampers sent anonymously. To this day, I always choose a family to give food to on the holidays. You've got to give back, or you're not worth anything. Mom scrubbed the floors at the Longshoreman Protective Union, or as she put it, 'cleaned the spit off the floors.' With that, and some assistance from social services, and the veterans' pension when it finally came, we got by."

When the four oldest, all girls, turned fifteen, they were routinely taken out of school and sent to work. Sarah remembers the principal coming into her classroom, taking her aside and saying, "C'mon Sarah, we've got a job for you now."

Her older sister worked for fifty cents an hour at a fish plant. Sarah replaced another sister at the local bakery, and that became a pattern: one would leave, and another sister would come of age and take over.

Sarah started out at sixty-eight cents an hour, which went up to eighty-six cents after a strike. Her mother would send one of the boys up on payday to pick up her cheque. Sarah was allowed ten cents a day to buy a Coke. "I used to hate her for doing that. I learned at a young age to resent her. I didn't know why she hated me, but she was very abusive, physically and mentally. I guess I was her scapegoat."

When her mother was pregnant with her, she'd suffered from toxemia, and she seemed to blame Sarah for that, and just about anything else that came along. One sister, with "more education than sense," says Sarah, was "cursed as a child. I know I was, and I know my mother cursed my brother when she was carrying him."

Sarah tells me, "All the time I was growing up, she'd call me a little slut, say I'd destroyed the family. She became very hard, very bitter. Here she'd married into a prosperous family, and yet she was faced with hardship with a husband in the Mental."

In Newfoundland, your "Nanny" is very important. Sarah felt very fortunate to have her grandmother in her life then, a loving, caring woman—her mother's mother—who taught her the right values, as well as showing her that she could be loved. But none of the children called their dad's mother anything but Grandmother Sharpe. "She was standoffish, with her pearls and diamonds. We used to see our cousins in nice dresses and coats while we went around in second-hand stuff."

Sarah's father was in and out of the Waterford. He used to get worse in the fall, his condition probably aggravated by his wife, who would do horrible things, such as force him to take all the kids—even the babies—down to the basement and give them beatings. Bones would be broken; the abuse was hard.

Sarah remembers taking her father back to the hospital one day, and him looking at her and saying it was the last time he'd go home. "I will never injure the heart, soul and mind of my children again," he told her. That was in August 1966. And he didn't come out again, not till Christmas of 1978.

"Only my older sister and I, out of all my family, have never abused our children," Sarah says.

We pull up in front of the Waterford. "Now I'm probably going to get emotional on you," Sarah warns me as we climb the stairs to the hospital. We're going to see the chapel that her father was instrumental in establishing. He was a deeply religious, spiritual man, who always slept with his window open just a little.

"I'd tell him, 'Dad, close the window, it's too cold.' And he'd say, 'Sarah, if God decides to take me tonight, I don't want my spirit to stay trapped in here.' I do the same thing now, leave my window open just enough."

He'd first been admitted in November 1953. He died on May 3, 1992. He spent a total of forty-nine years at the Waterford. Sarah's mother is still alive, but there's no closeness between them.

"I've started to see my mother a little better now, to imagine what she was feeling, what she was going through. They really loved each other, you know, loved each other till the day he died. Neither of them ever took their wedding rings off, neither of them ever went outside their marriage. Even sitting around here, my dad would say to her, if she'd been talking to another man, 'Oh my, you shouldn't be enticing people to look at you.' They'd send love letters back and forth, the years didn't seem to matter. It was a pure, honest and beautiful kind of love."

We stop at the wicket, like at a post office, where reception pages security to take us to the chapel. Noises assault us as we wait, loud moans and grunts and a kind of wailing; a few patients are scattered around, moving stiffly in the manner of the over-medicated.

When a polite and helpful security man leads us down the hospital corridors, a young patient trails behind us. He's supposed to get out today, though he shouldn't have been here in the first place, he tells us.

The guard unlocks the chapel and leaves us there, the three of us. Sarah goes immediately to a glass-encased plaque on the wall: inside it is a large pair of gold-plated scissors and below it an inscription:

Waterford Chapel Opening
October 16, 1981
Sister Laurentia Murray
Mr. Henry Sharpe

Sarah is indeed crying quietly, standing before this memory. The young man is watching her with a kind of awe. "My

God," he says to me. "She's some lucky she can cry. I've lost all my emotions."

When Sarah has regained her composure, we talk a little more, in this sanctuary.

She was married at eighteen, she tells me, to a fellow who was an alcoholic. He was abusive, mentally more than physically. "If he hit me, I'd hit him back. Dad was the first feminist I ever met. He would tell me, 'If a man ever hits you, hit him back.' He knew and could quote you the Charter of Rights and Freedoms. He even forced them here to let him go vote."

Sarah's first marriage lasted about fourteen years, with much of that time spent in Scarborough, Ontario. It was in Ontario that she was first exposed to real, naked poverty. She remembers her first glimpse of highrise public housing, and thinking, "Public housing isn't up in the sky like that." Driving around Sherbourne Street, and also in Parkdale in Toronto's west end, she saw her first crazies wandering the streets.

"We didn't have anything like that back home. There was Silly Willie, but that was it. The rest were inside."

IN 1993, THIS NEWFOUNDLANDER packed her bags and her courage and flew off to Geneva, to appear before a committee of the United Nations: the Committee on Social, Economic, and Cultural Rights, sponsored by the National Anti-Poverty Organization. Canada has to appear every few years to report on poverty in this country and how it's being dealt with. The official delegates had essentially claimed that there was no real poverty in our country, and Sarah was there to present the other side. It was intimidating.

"All I could think about was all the marble in the building; it was so beautiful, and so old. I'd never seen anything like that! And so many translators! Every language in the world." I grin, thinking they probably had to rush out and find yet another one, to translate St. John's into posh, flat English.

With other anti-poverty activists, Sarah presented a report called *The Right to an Adequate Standard of Living in the Land of Plenty*. She spoke of the "mental patients" abandoned to the street, of the lives of single mothers and the growing homeless population, the plight of aboriginal people in places like Davis Inlet.

"I wasn't really nervous, I just kept in my mind who I was doing this for. All the poor people who needed me to tell the international community that Canada was lying."

Like Doug in his testimony about the Christian Brothers at Mount Cashel, like Theresa in her court challenge of social services, Sarah told the truth, in a very public forum. The official Canadian delegates were furious. They felt sandbagged and were clearly unprepared to answer the report's allegations.

"We had Canada by the short hairs. There was no way they could disprove our presentations."

Sarah became poverty's whistle-blower.

LATER IN THE WEEK, I run into Matthew again in Bannerman Park, and he tells me that there are two ladies at Emmanuel House who've read at least one of my books and are dying to meet me. I promise I'll be over at ten the next morning.

Emmanuel House is welcoming—big and warm and kept in good repair. When I get there, there are four people waiting, sitting around the dining-room table. It would have looked like a committee meeting except for the presence of a heap of loose tobacco and an automatic rolling machine Matthew is operating. I'm introduced to, among others, a young woman in her thirties named Deborah Jackman. From 1990 to 1991 Deborah attended an outside program for sexual abuse survivors run out of Emmanuel.

There were sixteen children in Deborah's family. They lived, at first, in a small village called Grole, in a house with four big bedrooms, one of which was so large it held three double beds. She describes her mother as "a very angry slave," while her father was a fisherman and an alcoholic.

When Deborah was four or five, something happened to her in the storehouse where the men kept their gear. She remembers being surrounded by them. She remembers becoming hysterical, and her father coming in and beating her. Thinking back now, she suspects her father might have traded her to the men for a bottle.

Four sisters, including Deborah and her twin, were abused by one brother. Deborah thinks she was about twelve, he was sixteen, when he first came into her bedroom.

"We worked like dogs every day, but come night time, we were afraid to go to sleep."

The twins went to their oldest sister, Joan, who was more of a real mother to them than their own, and told her that the brother had moved on to the younger kids. Her response was: "Oh my God, don't say anything, it'll kill Mom and Dad."

Deborah then talked about it with her best friend, who was silent for a moment, then said: "My brother Edward and his friend give me money to stand in my nightgown next to the lamp."

The tiny village was due for resettlement. The provincial government in the late 1960s and early '70s felt it would be easier, cheaper and more convenient to provide resources and services if people were lumped together in larger communities. Barges were to carry residents' houses down to Harbour Breton, but the one Deborah and her family lived in was too large to be freighted. Instead, her dad bought an aunt's house in the new community of six hundred people, for $200. It was painfully small. Even to a little seven-year-old girl.

"My twin and I slept in a baby's crib, that's all there was for us. I still remember the night it broke." With the sharpness of old resentments, she adds, "Grandpa Taylor came with us, I remember well, and he got to have a whole bedroom to himself."

In Grole, the family had lived off the land, but that wasn't going to be so easy now. "They hadn't told us the new house was on a steep slope. My mother looked at it, and said 'How in the Lord Jesus Christ am I supposed to plant potatoes in that?'" And there was a need for money that hadn't been there before. The school expected different exercise books for every subject, sneakers for inside and sneakers for outside. She remembers her mother going a whole year without her false teeth, they'd been mislaid or lost somewhere, and the happy day she was digging in the potatoes and found them again.

The children loved to hear her laugh. "She was an extremely critical person, and a gossip. But we'd make her laugh playing Pentecost, after that religion came to our town. It was a small church, and there'd be all these uplifting songs, all this happy, happy, joy, joy and a little praying. Then the kids would be sent down to the gloomy basement for Sunday School, to learn about Jesus, but if you stuck it out they'd give you a little present at the end. I remember wanting the balloon with Jesus on it. People would get dipped and saved, and dipped and saved again. Mother would laugh along with us when we'd tell her what went on in the service, and she'd ask us: 'Did Grace give her testimony?' We all wanted to play Grace for her, she was the most dramatic Pentecost we knew. Mom would laugh such a hearty laugh, you'd want to embellish, falling on our knees with our hands in the air."

Deborah started experiencing panic attacks when she was only seven. "I felt like I was choking, in my throat. It was some bizarre when I think about it: they took me to a doctor, and he prescribed pills they'd hide in Jell-O pudding. It just grogged you out and dragged you down."

Still, she was fortunate in that the family that lived across the street, who were "severely poverty stricken and suffered as much as we did," had a little girl who became her new best friend. "She taught me everything. And we shoplifted like you can't believe, starting with little five-cent bars of Jersey Milk chocolate."

But early sexual abuse has a way of catching up to you, and Deborah started on a long and futile search for help. She began to show signs of mental illness and was put on the psychiatric ward at the hospital in Grand Falls.

"I remember overhearing some of the female patients talking, and I eavesdropped, and I heard one say, kind of lightly, how her uncle had molested her. I remember thinking, 'Oh my God!' I'd never had a word for what happened to me. So I adopted the same casual tone, joining in with the group, telling my own story."

She was always sent back home after her stays, and she says she now finds it ironic how happy she'd be to be returning to her family.

It seems like predators can smell out emotional vulnerability, and some of those predators are the very people that are supposed to be the helpers. Deborah blew the whistle on her psychiatrist, who was sexually abusing her, even though she wasn't sure what was really going on.

"I remember sitting with a nurse, and just losing it, throwing my purse across the room, and screaming at her that she had to listen to me, that I didn't know if what he was doing was right, but even if it was, I didn't want him to do it any more."

She was fortunate, in a way, as anyone knows who has sat through trials or hearings, that he was arrogant enough, when confronted by the head of the hospital, to admit what he'd done, rationalizing it by saying "She wanted it." According to him, so did the other half dozen patients he'd abused, women who came forward once Deborah had accused him.

It's a difficult road for Deborah, trying to piece her life together, trying to move on. She's taken up public performance art, is on social assistance, which gives her $318 every two weeks, and lives in a small apartment above a women's centre. She's started self-help and advocacy groups and is still able to find peer support and refuge in this sprawling house.

IN ST. JOHN'S, I LEARNED that men have been right all along: size doesn't matter. The smallest city can aspire to world-class status, and can also be plagued with world-class concerns: homelessness, panhandling, kid gangs, drugs and gambling.

Here, people are now seeing the consequences of the sexual abuse that went on in surrounding communities and in their own back yard for years. Silence, shame and isolation are factors that helped abuse take root and grow. That silence has been broken, but the effects are still being felt by those who still live with the shame and the self-blame.

People here hope that more openness, more awareness, might have eradicated the problem, saved the next generation. That may be so, but a large part of that success depends on how we salvage the adult individuals whose lives were damaged, so that their children can grow in innocence and love.

Isolation and silence and abuse can happen on the most neighbourly residential street in the biggest city and go ignored forever. Perhaps St. John's, because of its smallness, can succcessfully accomplish healing and prevention by engaging its community in dialogue and understanding.

There are no happy endings, even in fairy-tale towns.

EPILOGUE

TIMES ARE TOUGH. FEW people feel very secure in their jobs; the bloodletting, downsizing era isn't quite behind us. We don't trust our employers, don't trust governments that seem to waste thousands, even millions of tax dollars and then come to us with add-ons like the GST and user fees. We can't trust the sun, can't trust the air we breathe, can't even trust the water that comes out of our taps.

Our university-educated children are burdened with the debt of student loans, hard to pay off when you're working at McDonald's. Many have moved back home, unable to provide for themselves the lifestyle they enjoyed growing up. We worry about them, about their future. And we worry about ourselves as we age and become frail, vulnerable and dependent.

We are angry. And we have an absolute right to be.

When people turn up on our streets, staking out bits of sidewalk, taking over our parks, making homes out of the entries to businesses and apartment buildings, we take refuge—most of us—in the illusion that their homelessness is a "lifestyle choice." And when we're confronted by squeegee kids, or panhandlers on every block, we become furious that we, who are already feeling besieged, are being asked to pay for their choices. It's the same fury we feel when we're asked to pay to support a single woman, barely out of childhood herself, to raise her children. Our right as citizens to not be bothered by these people, our right to worry only about our own futures, is being infringed upon everywhere we look.

We want panhandling controlled. We want our sidewalks back.

We hear from the traditional Left, the self-styled champions of social services and safety nets, that the problem is caused by slashes to services, and they lead the chant, Give us back our programs. But the truth is, of course, that these are problems that were festering long before we became a leaner, meaner, more competitive country. It takes years of living in poverty—years of failed, inadequate and inept interventions—to land someone on the street.

Sometimes, it is the entirely predictable outcome of generations of neglect, of abuse, of hunger.

If we as a society had set out on a deliberate strategy to

create, reinforce and maintain environments, like mushroom factories, where various reactive pathologies could take root and flourish, we could not have achieved more success. The child born into poverty, innocently coming into the world, must bear all the consequences of our inadequate meddling in the lives of its parents, and quite likely, their parents' parents before them.

An infant born into an impoverished, troubled family will likely experience abuse even before he or she utters a first word. Parents who were themselves subject to a wide gamut of abuse and neglect as children, who've never experienced a different way of relating, of disciplining, of making children feel valued, who must live with the daily stresses of barely getting by, are ill equipped to give what they themselves have never received.

That child will learn that words like father, mother, grandparents mean very different things from the emotionally loaded, Hallmark versions generally accepted in society. That child will grow up taking responsibility for the failures of his parents, believing himself to be "bad," worthy only of the punishment that is a more steady diet than whatever food is on offer.

Whether the abuse is physical, sexual, or mental, the odds are abuse will be there. How the child reacts to that abuse will determine what system he becomes attached to.

It is a time-honoured tradition that kids in trouble tend to "act out," to thrash around, looking for help or comfort or some sense of self-worth. We don't tolerate that any more.

School boards confronted with difficult situations adopt zero-tolerance policies towards violence that remove the kids from the school, cull these children from the ranks of the successful. Children who already believe they're bad and the source of all the problems at home have this reinforced at school—good children from good families must be protected from them.

The rejected child, still lost in behaviours that bring punishment rather than rescue, has some limited options to make himself feel better. Drugs, of course, will be rampant in his neighbourhood, an artificial and temporary way to fill in the blanks that crater his existence. Instant feel-good. Or he or she might simply go mad. Crack under the weight, get captured by the mental health system and lead a different, drug-controlled existence legitimized by a scientific-sounding diagnosis.

Or go bad. Take what you want. Take what you feel you need. There are boot camps and prisons filled with those who take this route.

The men and women selling and using heroin, morphine, cocaine on a Vancouver street corner were very familiar to me, very much like me and the others in my community who, faced with a cancelled life, try to find something to subdue the pain. In Edmonton and Winnipeg, starting out poor means ending up poor, and labelled with some form of societal deviancy. In Montreal, the road to misery starts very young, and hardens and shapes a reality with no exits.

Our common ground is our disenfranchisement, our

poverty, our inability to see any reason why we are here.

What makes your life worth living? What would cause you to trade it in for a chemical hit? What would it take for you to accept a no-life alternative and still go on? And what loyalty or concern would you feel for the city, province or country that watched you fall so far, and then blamed you for it?

We know, to paraphrase Orwell, that some Canadians are more equal, more worthy than others. The rest?

The rest are in another country, not quite Canada, not quite civilized, certainly not developed. A country of the poor and lost, within a country, a land, of plenty.

EVERYTHING I HAVE SEEN and learned and felt in my long journey as a mental health advocate for twenty years, everything I've learned and felt and discovered in the different communities of the poor—from Vancouver to St. John's—since I started this book, has led me to some important conclusions.

We've made poverty a crime in the 1990s. A crime that requires strict punishment and new solutions. Like cutbacks, because we were giving too much. Like workfare, because everyone who wants to work in this country can find a job. It's Canada, after all, the best country in the world.

A Report Card on Poverty and the Canadian Welfare State, issued in January 1998 by the National Anti-Poverty Organization, states:

Between 1990 and 1996 there was a rapid erosion of all three elements of the Canadian welfare state. First, there were growing inequities in access to both health care and post-secondary education for low-income Canadians, resulting from a significant decline in real public funding for these services. Second, there was an approximately 40 per cent cut in Employment Insurance (EI)–benefits ($6 billion annually) over the 1990–1996 period. Deep cuts in EI, combined with changes in the labour market, have resulted in a sharp fall in the proportion of the unemployed who are able to receive EI benefits. . . . Third, many provinces in recent years have tightened eligibility requirements for social assistance and/or cut benefit rates.

The number of poor people rose considerably over the 1990–1996 period. By 1996 poor Canadians were much worse off in economic terms than they were in 1990. They were also significantly worse off in comparison to more affluent Canadians. . . .

According to Statistics Canada, the richest 20 per cent of Canadians saw their average incomes increase $2,000 between 1995 and 1996, while the poorest 20 per cent saw their average incomes fall $500.

WHAT MOST OF US suspect is true: all the money poured into social services over the years has not accomplished what it should have, what it could have. In Vancouver, we exchange hypodermic needles, over two and a half million last year; in Montreal, over the same period, forty thousand hot dogs were handed out to street kids. In Toronto, we hand out mats to the homeless who make it to the Out of the Cold program, and sleeping bags to those who remain out in the snow. Is this the best we can do?

We have created and sustained a dual dependency—that of worker and client—by fostering increasing numbers of agencies and workers and programs and bureaucracies that are all supported from the public purse, without properly determining whether they will meet the needs of those in the greatest distress. We have allowed our agencies to create a caste system whereby the "deserving," "hopeful" and "inoffensive" poor— those who are able to follow the rules—are allowed access to limited social services, while the rest are left to their fate. Accountability is lacking, true accountability based on the real impact these services have on the quality of life of all the individuals in their target groups.

There are more traps, and harsher consequences, lying in wait for the poor than for any other class. And there are helping systems in place for every trap except the biggest one: poverty itself. Mental health, addictions, corrections, welfare and disability, women's shelters, Children's Aid—all are overburdened, all creating and sustaining their own caseloads. All ensuring, by their very nature, a revolving-door syndrome.

Even more damaging are the blinkers each helping system seems to adopt. Staying within their own narrow world view, their own specialty, their own concern often means missing or turning a blind eye to the obvious.

And when agencies fail to allow their clients any portion of the power to determine how they are served, there can be no quality of service. Somewhere along the line, problems replace people, and the clients' real existence and adult struggles become even more obscured. For the worker, the problems get tiresome, seemingly unresolvable, as case loads continue to grow, as options shrink. Invisible issues, such as power differentials, stay hidden. Only the client knows they are there. The effect of all this is simply to reinforce all the negatives that brought the client into the agency in the first place, all the side-effects of poverty and the traps laid out for those caught up in it.

Low self-esteem. I wish there was a stronger term that could be used to explain what those who have grown up with abuse feel about themselves, because ultimately that bears the heaviest impact on their lives.

Inability to affect their environment. At home, at the agencies where help is offered, passivity is the order of the day.

Dependence. Being seen as merely a collection of problems that need fixing does nothing to foster independence. Caring and attention—the worker likely being the only person in the client's life who is, or seems to be, paying attention to the daily dramas—is in itself new and addictive. To keep that caring, to foster the illusion, more and more problems are presented, resulting in less and less individual effort to step out of them. Need is emphasized, not personal strength.

Lack of education, employment and job skills. This is a given, and it ensures continuing isolation and continuing poverty.

Across Canada, we make stiffer rules against panhandling, while in Alberta we ensure that those cut from the welfare rolls have nowhere to turn, nothing to live on. In developing countries, we are told the birth rate remains high because of the parents' need to be sure some of their children will survive into adulthood, to take care of them in their old age, to help work the land; in Canada, some of the poor keep having children because the ones they had keep getting taken away by children's service organizations.

We are punishing the beaten, rather than looking at how we could revamp a bloated and often irrelevant system of social services that has played a large part in creating the universe of pain that belongs to the poor.

We are making the poor pay for our failures—through our governments, through our systems, through our willful ignorance.